The Dog Breed Handbook

The Dog Breed Handbook

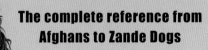

The complete reference from Afghans to Zande Dogs

Joan Palmer

CHARTWELL
BOOKS, INC.

A QUARTO BOOK

This edition published in 2009 by
CHARTWELL BOOKS, INC.
A division of BOOK SALES, INC.
276 Fifth Avenue Suite 206
New York, New York 10001
USA

ISBN-13: 978-0-7858-2558-6
ISBN-10: 0-7858-2558-4

Conceived, designed, and produced by
Quarto Publishing plc
The Old Brewery
6 Blundell Street
London N7 9BH

QUAR: DBR

Editor: Michelle Pickering
Art editor: Anna Knight
Designer: Penny Dawes
Assistant art director: Penny Cobb
Photographer: Paul Forrester
Art director: Moira Clinch
Publisher: Piers Spence

With special thanks to Rose Forrester
for researching the dog breeds and to
Jimmy Forrester for making friends
with all the dogs and their owners.

Manufactured by Universal Graphics
Pte Ltd, Singapore
Printed by Midas Printing International
Ltd, China

Contents

Working Breeds 52

Herding Breeds 74

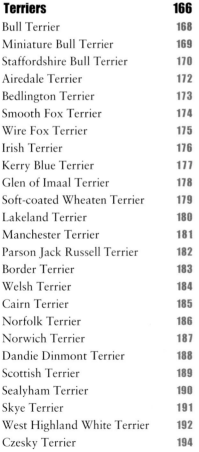

Introduction

The relationship between dogs and humankind has long been a special one. From the giant Saint Bernard rescuing mountaineers in the Swiss Alps to the pampered Pekingese of the Chinese imperial court, dogs have been blessing humans with their unique skills and companionship for millennia.

Every dog is beautiful in its own way, and the very wide range of breeds of pedigree dogs existing today means that every dog lover can indulge his or her particular preference. However, always remember that each breed of dog has its own distinct characteristics—looks, size, character, and temperament—so it is essential to get as much information as possible about all the different breeds to enable you to select the right dog to meet your requirements. Remember that looks can be deceiving: some big, macho-looking

dogs are great big softies, and some small breeds are famed for ill-humor.

This book outlines the characteristics of over 160 different breeds to help you find out which ones are really suitable for you. If you make your choice with care, the partnership between dog and owner will be a happy and long-lasting one.

Showing dogs

The first dogs were bred selectively for a specific purpose, such as herding livestock or dispelling vermin. By the middle of the 19th century, with interest in dogs steadily increasing, the need for a group system became apparent. The current system has generally been developed to take into account the type of work, if any, and the size of breeds.

All breeds placed by their national kennel club within a specific group are given a breed standard. This sets out a standard of excellence for representatives of that breed, and includes such modifications as ideal height and/or weight, desirable colors, conformation points, and so on. There are often slight differences in what is deemed ideal from country to country.

Buying a dog that will turn into a good show dog can never be guaranteed, because it is generally not possible to determine a dog's full potential until it is several months old. However, familiarity with the different characteristics required for the breed should give you a reasonable chance of obtaining a good show dog.

The Löwchen, or Little Lion Dog, was established in France and Spain as long ago as the 16th century.

How to use this book

Care requirements are provided
for each breed (see below)

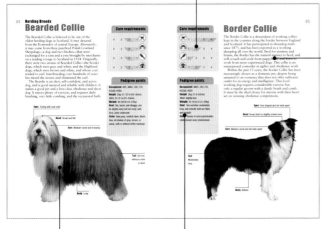

The introductory text
describes the background
of the breed and how it
developed, followed by
advice on the breed's
character and care

A head-to-tail description
is given for each breed

Pedigree points provides specific information about the
size, coat, and color standards required for the breed

Care requirements

The care requirements box provides an at-a-glance
reference for how to look after each breed of dog.
The scales in the chart range from one to four, with
one being the least requirement and four the greatest.

Care requirements

| 4 | 3 | 2 | 1 | |

Exercise indicates the amount of
exercise a particular breed requires

Feeding specifies the quantity of
food that should be given

Grooming indicates the amount
of grooming needed

Space gives a guide to the amount
of room the breed requires

*The Miniature Pinscher
makes an ideal family pet,
requiring only moderate
exercise and minimal
grooming, space, and food.*

Canine Associations

A total of 51 countries have registries for dog breeds, each one concerned with the classification and registration of dogs, setting breed standards, and holding dog shows.

CANADIAN KENNEL CLUB—CKC
- Sporting Breeds
- Terriers
- Non-sporting Breeds
- Hounds
- Toy Breeds
- Working Breeds
- Herding Breeds
- Miscellaneous Class

AMERICAN KENNEL CLUB—AKC
- Non-sporting Breeds
- Working Breeds
- Herding Breeds
- Sporting Breeds
- Hounds
- Terriers
- Toy Breeds

KENNEL UNION OF SOUTHERN AFRICA—KUSA
- Hounds
- Gundogs
- Terriers
- Utility Breeds
- Herding Breeds
- Working Breeds
- Toy Breeds

SCANDINAVIAN KENNEL CLUBS
- Spitz Breeds
- Trailing and Hunting Breeds
- Gundogs
- Guard and Working Breeds
- Terriers
- Sighthounds
- Non-sporting and Companion Breeds
- Toy Breeds

Féderation Cynologique Internationale—FCI
- Sheepdogs and Cattle Dogs
- Guard and Working Breeds
- Terriers
- Dachshunds
- Spitz Types/Hounds for Larger Game
- Scenthounds/Hounds for Smaller Game
- Pointers
- Gundogs
- Companions and Toys
- Sighthounds/Greyhounds

(BRITISH) KENNEL CLUB—KC (GB)
- Hounds
- Gundogs
- Terriers
- Utility Breeds
- Working Breeds
- Toy Breeds

AUSTRALIAN NATIONAL KENNEL CLUB—ANKC
- Toy Breeds
- Gundogs
- Hounds
- Working Breeds
- Utility Breeds
- Non-sporting Breeds

Breed Groups

Breed groups are of great help, not only in categorizing the breeds for exhibition purposes, but also in aiding the purchaser to select the breed best suited to the purpose that he or she has in mind, be it a children's pet, hunting dog, or guard.

Non-sporting breeds

This is the category from which many pet dogs are selected. The breeds may well have performed some task in the past, but in the main they are now the dogs whose sole purpose in life is to be a companion to their owners, from the Dalmatian, a former carriage dog, to the more sedate Chow Chow (left).

Working breeds

This group covers the traditional guards and workers—rescue, sled, and draft dogs, and those favored by the armed services, such as the Rottweiler (above). Bred to work, most are happiest when they are doing the job for which they are bred or at least when in an environment where their abilities will not go to waste.

Herding breeds

The breeds in this group were originally developed to herd and protect sheep, such as the German Shepherd Dog (above), cattle, and other stock. Many are still used by shepherds and farmers, but they are also extremely adaptable as pets, often taking it upon themselves to herd the family together.

Gundogs

In this group are the pointers, retrievers (shown above is the Golden Retriever), and spaniels—all gundogs used variously to detect, flush out, and retrieve game. Usually gentle natured, many dogs in this category have the dual role of huntsman's dog and family pet.

Hounds

Hounds are often divided into those that hunt by scent, such as the Bloodhound and Beagle (above), and those that rely on their keen eyesight, like the Greyhound and the Saluki. Hounds are good natured but have a propensity to roam. Many hounds are kept in packs, in outside kennels, rather than living indoors.

Terriers

These dogs were bred to go to ground, to hunt vermin, and bolt the fox from its lair. Energetic, sporting, and sometimes noisy, most terriers are affectionate by nature, but they can be nippy. The West Highland White Terrier (above) is a friendly and very popular dog.

Toy breeds

Do not be fooled by the fact that the traditional ladies' lapdogs, such as the Pomeranian (above), come within this category. Most are splendid guards, keenly intelligent, energetic, affectionate, if somewhat possessive, and courageous to the point of stupidity.

Terminology

If you take a random selection of pure-bred dogs, you will notice that their heads, ears, eyes, tails, and colors differ. As many new breeds have developed over the years, and continue to develop and become recognized as official breeds by the kennel clubs, it has become necessary to standardize the way in which all these differences are described.

To the inexperienced eye, or to the owner who buys a pure-bred dog purely as a pet, minor variations from the "standard" may be unimportant, but for showing purposes, every detail counts in assessing a dog as a representative of its type. The special terminology used today has been developed to encompass all aspects of a dog's appearance and conformation, and makes interesting reading for any dog owner.

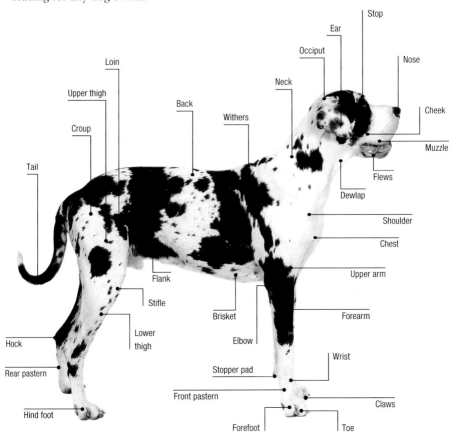

Stop

Ear

Occiput

Nose

Loin

Neck

Cheek

Upper thigh

Back

Withers

Muzzle

Croup

Flews

Tail

Dewlap

Shoulder

Chest

Upper arm

Flank

Forearm

Stifle

Brisket

Hock

Lower thigh

Elbow

Wrist

Rear pastern

Stopper pad

Front pastern

Claws

Hind foot

Forefoot

Toe

Heads

There are three skull types—mesoticephalic, brachycephalic, and dolichocephalic—that describe the basic shape of the head, plus many subtypes.

Mesoticephalic
Medium proportions of width to length (Irish Water Spaniel)

Brachycephalic
Short and compressed with a rounded cranium (Pekingese)

Dolichocephalic
Long and narrow with shallow cranium (Borzoi)

Clean
Free from wrinkles or lumps (Golden Retriever)

Balanced
Skull and foreface equal in length (English Springer Spaniel)

Rectangular
Slightly domed (West Highland White Terrier)

Blocky
Square or cube-like (Staffordshire Bull Terrier)

Pear-shaped
Rounded skull with tapering muzzle (Bedlington Terrier)

Apple
Domed and rounded (Chihuahua)

Egg-shaped
Free from hollowing to end of muzzle (Bull Terrier)

Otter
Broad, flat skull and short, strong muzzle (Border Terrier)

Fox-like
Short foreface with pointed nose and ears (Schipperke)

Ears

Ears are described in terms of their shape and how they hang. In some countries, several breeds have their ears cropped to make them stand erect.

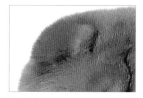

Hooded

Small and erect, but tilted forward (Chow Chow)

Bat

Erect, broad at base, with rounded tip (French Bulldog)

Button

Ear flap folding forward (Irish Terrier)

Filbert-shaped

Hazelnut-shaped (Bedlington Terrier)

Semi-drop/semi-pricked

Just the tips break and fall forward (Shetland Sheepdog)

Drop

Ends fold or drop forward (English Cocker Spaniel)

Pricked

Erect and generally pointed (German Shepherd Dog)

Hound

Triangular, rounded, and flap folding forward (Beagle)

Heart-shaped

Shaped like a heart (Pekingese)

V-shaped/triangular

Usually carried in dropped position (Hungarian Vizsla)

Rose

Small drop ear that folds over and back (Pug)

Eyes

The terminology for eyes is based on the shape of the eyes and how they are set in the skull. The position in the skull affects the dog's field of vision.

Goggly
*Round and protruding
(Brussels Griffon)*

Circular
*As round as possible
(Smooth Fox Terrier)*

Oblique
*Angled from ear to muzzle (Miniature
Wire-haired Dachshund)*

Pig
Very small and hard (Pug)

Almond
*Almond-shaped
(German Shepherd Dog)*

Globular
*Appear to protrude, but not when
seen in profile (Chihuahua)*

Haw
*Third membrane in the inside corner
of the eye (Bloodhound)*

Triangular
*Set in triangular-shaped tissue
(Afghan Hound)*

Deep set
*Sunk well down in the eye sockets
(Chow Chow)*

Tails

Tail descriptions refer to length, shape, and position. In some countries, the tails of some breeds are docked to make them appear more aggressive or to prevent damage.

Flag
Long and carried high (Beagle)

Whip
Carried stiffly straight and pointed (Bull Terrier)

Otter
Thick at the root, round and tapering toward tip (Labrador Retriever)

Spike
Short, thick, and tapering (Lakeland Terrier)

Sickle
Carried out and up in a semicircle (Affenpinscher)

Crank
Carried down and resembling a crank (Italian Segugio)

Brush
Like the brush of a fox (Alaskan Malamute)

Squirrel
Carried up and curving forward (Chow Chow)

Bobtail
Naturally tailless or docked very short (Old English Sheepdog)

Kink
Sharply bent (Lhasa Apso)

Curled
Curled over onto spine or one side (Finnish Spitz)

Screw
Short and twisted in a spiral fashion (French Bulldog)

Coat Colors

The standards for some breeds allow many different coat colors, while other breeds have very little variety.

Roan
(Welsh Corgi Cardigan)

Particolor
(Swedish Vallhund)

Belton
(English Setter)

Grizzle
(Old English Sheepdog)

Piebald
(Dalmation)

Brindle
(Greyhound)

Tricolor
(Beagle)

Wheaten
(Soft-coated Wheaten Terrier)

Blue
(Great Gascony Blue)

Red
(Irish Setter)

Black and tan
(Hamiltonstövare)

Harlequin
(Great Dane)

Choosing a Dog

Ownership of a dog is a serious undertaking. It requires a long-term commitment, keeping in mind that some breeds, the Miniature Poodle for instance, may live for 17 years or more. Twelve years is the average canine lifespan, during which time the dog must be fed, exercised, and groomed, receive veterinary attention for accidents and illnesses, and be taken into consideration whenever its owner is planning to be away from home for more than a matter of hours.

First, it is important that the decision to buy a dog has the approval of both partners; likewise with the choice of breed. Second, never buy a dog on face value. Always check whether its abilities, temperament, and requirements are suitable for the role that you have in mind, and your circumstances. For instance, you may live in an apartment or in a house, in the town or in the country, and your choice of breed should take this into account. In the case of a large, powerful breed and/or one that needs a great deal of exercise, you must be certain that you and/or your partner have the physical strength to control it.

By now you will have realized that study of the canine groups helps the dog buyer to narrow down the choice to

Feeding

The cost element should play a role in your choice of dog. Remember that large breeds and working dogs cost considerably more to maintain, in food terms, than smaller ones.

Canned meat

Complete dried food

Fresh meat

Semi-moist meat

Puppy mixer meal

Dog biscuits

Rawhide chew

Chew sticks

Vitamin treats

breeds that fall within the most suitable category. In each case, you should find a number of varieties from which to make a choice. It should not be too difficult to find several breeds that, for example, combine the role of sporting dog and/or guard with that of a family pet, or that could, if you wish, be kenneled outdoors, mindful that most pet dogs share their owners' home, but that many large, thick-coated dogs come to no harm outside.

Puppy health check

Carry out the following checks to make sure that the puppy of your choice is healthy before finalizing the purchase.

Body Pick up the puppy to check that it does not object or show signs of pain; its body should be firm and relaxed.

Ears Lift the ear flap and check that the ear canal is dry and clean.

Mouth Open the mouth gently and check that the tongue and gums are pink.

Eyes The eyes should be clear and bright, and there should be no signs of discharge.

Coat Run your hand against the grain of the coat to check for sores and the black dust caused by fleas.

Tail Check under the tail that there is no staining, which would indicate diarrhea.

Dog Care

Each breed of dog will have different care requirements. The majority of fanciers are only expert in preparing their own chosen breed, and perhaps one or two others. Only professional dog groomers could, for example, advise on the bathing, trimming, scissoring, and grooming of all the breeds recognized by the American Kennel Club.

Most people have a preference for a long- or a short-coated animal, and even sometimes for a particular color. Remember, however, that the long-coated animal is likely to need far more time spent on grooming than the short-coated one, and that a light-colored dog, for instance the Dalmatian, is going to shed hairs that will be apparent on the sitting-room carpet.

Grooming equipment

It is sensible when buying a puppy to discuss with the breeder the basic equipment you will need for grooming.

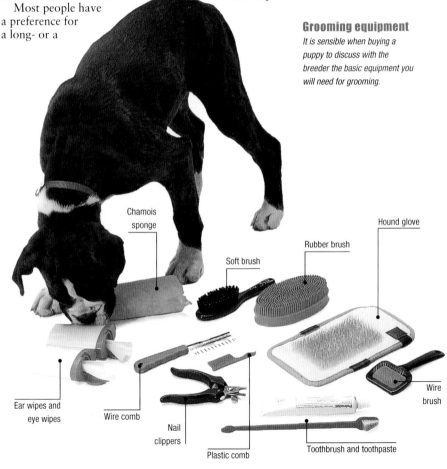

Chamois sponge

Hound glove

Rubber brush

Soft brush

Wire brush

Ear wipes and eye wipes

Wire comb

Nail clippers

Plastic comb

Toothbrush and toothpaste

Special effects

While quite a number of breeds have to be hand-stripped, using fingers and/or a stripping knife, to give the coat the desired effect for the show ring, these same breeds are often clipped instead when they are kept solely as domestic pets.

Smooth-coated breeds, such as the Staffordshire Bull Terrier, Boston Terrier, and French Bulldog, need only be groomed every day or two using a short, bristle brush; the German Shepherd Dog and many of the spaniels and retrievers need daily grooming using a bristle brush and a comb; those breeds that need particular coat care and regular visits to the grooming parlor for clipping, stripping, and, perhaps, scissoring, include the Airedale Terrier, Bichon Frise, the Schnauzers, and the Poodles.

It must be emphasized, therefore, that if time and expense are a consideration, you would be well advised to think in terms of a smooth, short-coated breed.

Routine grooming jobs

To keep your dog in the best possible condition, carry out the following checks on the dog's ears, eyes, teeth, and nails in addition to grooming the coat.

Ears Check the ears and ear flaps for any sign of wax or an unpleasant smell, which could be signs of canker. Ear swabs are available, or use absorbent cotton moistened with olive oil. Take immense care never to probe the ear too deeply.

Eyes Check the eyes for any inflammation and watering, and for opacity in the cornea. For routine care, it is possible to buy eye swabs specially formulated to clean the discharge often found around the eye area. Alternately, wipe away stains with cotton dipped in lukewarm water or cold tea.

Nails If your dog gets plenty of roadwork, its nails should wear down naturally. If not, they will need to be trimmed with veterinary clippers about every 3 months. The veterinarian will undertake this task.

Teeth Clean your dog's teeth with canine toothpaste. It is also sensible to take your dog to the veterinarian for regular scaling. This is particularly important in the case of toy breeds, which can lose their teeth at an early age.

Non-sporting Breeds

Bulldog

The Bulldog's proud ancestry can be traced back to the Molossus, the fighting dog named from an ancient Greek tribe, the Molossi. As its name suggests, it was bred to bait bulls. According to one story, this "sport" commenced in Britain in 1204 or thereabouts, when Lord Stamford of Lincolnshire in England was greatly amused by the sight of some butchers dogs tormenting a bull. This gave his Lordship the idea of providing a field in which bull-baiting tournaments might take place on condition that the butcher would provide one bull a year for the "sport." Later, pits were set up in various parts of Britain where dogs would also fight other dogs.

When bull-baiting became illegal in 1835, the Bulldog was in danger of extinction. Fortunately, however, a Mr Bill George continued to breed Bulldogs and, in 1875, the first specialist club for the breed was formed, known as the Bulldog Club Incorporated. This was followed in 1891 by the London Bulldog Society, which still holds its annual meeting at Crufts Dog Show.

Despite its fearsome appearance, the Bulldog is now a gentle, good-natured dog. It adores children and makes a delightful pet. The only grooming it requires is a daily run through with a stiff brush and a rub-down. Care must be taken that it is not over-exerted in hot weather.

The Bulldog's shoulders are broad, sloping, and deep. They are also very powerful and muscular, giving the appearance of having been tacked on to its body.

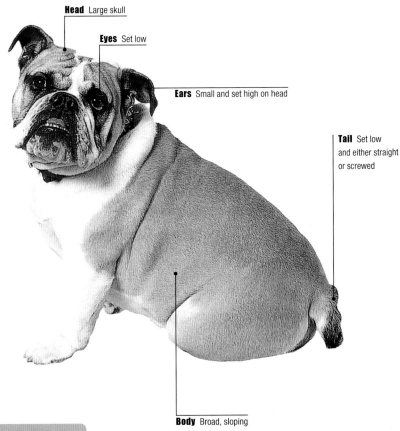

Head Large skull

Eyes Set low

Ears Small and set high on head

Tail Set low and either straight or screwed

Body Broad, sloping shoulders

Pedigree points

Recognized AKC, ANKC, CKC, FCI, KC(GB), KUSA
Weight *Dog:* 50–55 lb (22.5–25kg)
Bitch: 40–50 lb (18–22.5kg)
Coat Short, smooth, close, and finely textured
Color Uniform color or with black mask or muzzle; reds, red brindle, piebald; black undesirable

Care requirements

	1	2	3	4
	1	2	3	4
	1	2	3	4
	1	2	3	4

Non-sporting Breeds

French Bulldog

The French Bulldog is obviously a descendant of small bulldogs, but it is not known whether these were English dogs taken to France by Nottingham laceworkers in the 19th century or dogs imported to France from Spain. Small English Bulldog ancestry is generally accepted, despite the discovery of an ancient bronze plaque of a dog bearing an unmistakable likeness to the French Bulldog and inscribed: "Dogue de Burgos, España 1625."

This breed is a popular and easy dog to show. It is good natured, affectionate, and courageous, and usually gets on well with children and other pets. Owners must become accustomed to its gentle snuffling, and be aware that this flat-nosed breed should not be exercised in hot weather. The "Frenchie" is easy to groom, requiring just a daily brush and a rub-down with a silk handkerchief, or piece of toweling, to make its coat shine. The facial creases should be lubricated to prevent soreness.

Care requirements

Pedigree points

Recognized AKC, ANKC, CKC, FCI, KC(GB), KUSA
Height 12 in (30cm)
Weight *Dog:* 28 lb (12.5kg)
Bitch: 24 lb (11kg)
Coat Short, smooth, close, and finely textured
Color Brindle, piebald, or fawn

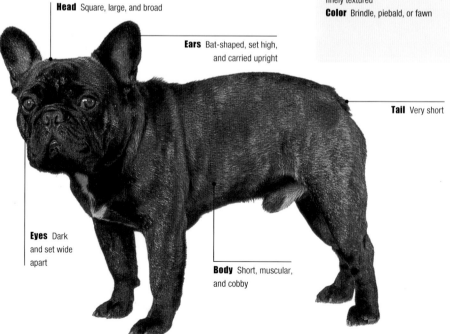

Head Square, large, and broad

Ears Bat-shaped, set high, and carried upright

Tail Very short

Eyes Dark and set wide apart

Body Short, muscular, and cobby

Boston Terrier

The Boston Terrier, formerly the American Bull Terrier, derives from a crossbred Bulldog/Terrier that was imported into the United States from Britain in 1865. Barnard's Tom, the first example of the breed with the desired screw tail, was bred in Boston, Massachusetts, and registered with the American Kennel Club in 1893. The breed takes its name from the city where it was developed.

The Boston Terrier is a lively, intelligent dog and a loving pet. It is easy to look after and requires little grooming. However, it is difficult to obtain a show specimen with the right markings—ideally, a white muzzle, even a white blaze over the head and down the collar, breast, and forelegs below the elbows.

Care requirements

1 2 3 4

1 2 3 4

1 2 3 4

1 2 3 4

Pedigree points

Recognized AKC, CKC, FCI, KC(GB)
Weight Divided by classes
Lightweight: under 15 lb (7kg)
Middleweight: under 20 lb (9kg)
Heavyweight: under 25 lb (11.5kg)
Coat Short and smooth
Color Brindle with white markings, black with white markings, but brindle with white markings preferred

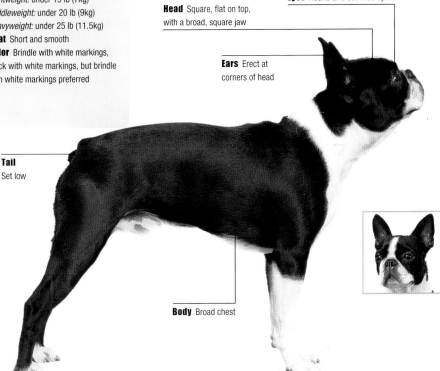

Eyes Round and set wide apart

Head Square, flat on top, with a broad, square jaw

Ears Erect at corners of head

Tail Set low

Body Broad chest

Dalmatian

The Dalmatian is named after Dalmatia on the Adriatic coast, but it is in Britain that the modern breed became well established. Heads would turn as a carriage of the British aristocracy went by with an elegant Dalmatian trotting alongside the horses. Although already popular in Britain, the Dalmatian's registrations doubled following the filming in 1959 of Dodie Smith's book, *101 Dalmatians*. The breed's friendly character and elegant appearance have made it popular as a pet and show dog worldwide.

This affectionate and energetic dog quickly becomes a family favorite. It requires plenty of exercise and a daily brushing but does tend to shed white hairs, which does not endear the breed to the houseproud. However, its intelligence and equable temperament should make up for this small failing.

Care requirements

4	3	2	1	🐕
4	3	2	1	🥣
4	3	2	1	🪮
4	3	2	1	🏠

Pedigree points

Recognized AKC, ANKC, CKC, FCI, KC(GB), KUSA
Height 19–23 in (47.5–58.5cm)
Weight 50–55 lb (22.5–25kg)
Coat Short, fine, dense, and close; sleek and glossy in appearance
Color Pure white ground color with round and well-defined black or liver brown spots, as evenly distributed as possible; spots on extremities smaller than those on body

Eyes Set moderately far apart

Head Long with flat skull

Ears Medium-sized and set high

Body Deep chest

Tail Long and carried with a slight upward curve

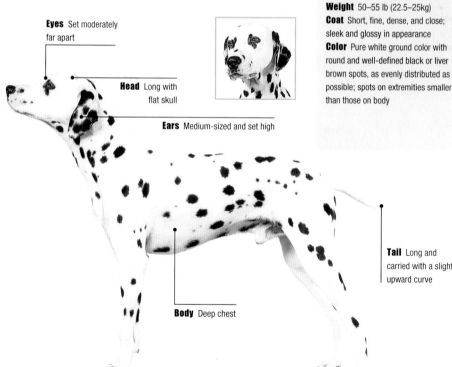

Care requirements

- 1 2 3 4
- 1 2 3 4
- 1 2 3 4
- 1 2 3 4

Pedigree points

Recognized AKC, ANKC, CKC, FCI, KC(GB), KUSA

Height *Dog:* 18½–19½ in (46–49cm)
Bitch: 17½–18½ in (44–46cm)

Weight 33 lb (15kg)

Coat Tight, hard, and wiry with a soft undercoat

Color Pure black (white markings on head, chest, and legs undesirable), or pepper and salt; darker facial mask is desirable

Standard Schnauzer

The Standard Schnauzer is the oldest of three varieties of Schnauzer, the others being the Miniature and Giant. Its origins are obscure. Some say that it was a cross between two now extinct breeds, the Beaver Dog of the Middle Ages and a rough-coated dog, perhaps a terrier, that was kept to dispel vermin. Others think that it evolved from the extinct Schafer Pudel and the Wire-haired German Pinscher. Others believe that it is descended from drovers dogs, including the Bouvier des Flandres to which it bears a close resemblance.

The Schnauzer is an attractive, robust, intelligent, and playful dog that makes a good companion and is generally good with children. It enjoys plenty of exercise, and its wiry coat needs a certain amount of stripping and plucking. Pet dogs can be clipped but this will spoil the coat for showing, so owners wishing to exhibit are advised to discuss grooming with the breeder at the time of purchase.

Eyes Dark and oval-shaped

Head Strong and of good length

Ears Set high

Tail Set and carried high, and characteristically docked to three joints

Body Chest moderately broad

Giant Schnauzer

The Giant Schnauzer was for many years known as the Münchener Dog, because it originated from an area near Munich. It is believed to have evolved from crosses between smooth-coated drovers dogs and rough-coated shepherd dogs, as well as black Great Danes and the Bouvier des Flandres. It worked as a cattle dog until the need for such an animal declined. Not as popular as the Standard and Miniature varieties, the Giant Schnauzer might have become extinct had it not proved itself an excellent guard dog in World War I.

This intelligent dog makes a good-natured companion that requires a fair amount of exercise. It needs little grooming other than stripping and plucking. The coat may also be clipped but this will spoil it for showing, so it is best to discuss grooming with the breeder at the time of purchase.

Care requirements

| 4 | 3 | 2 | 1 |

Pedigree points

Recognized AKC, ANKC, CKC, FCI, KC(GB), KUSA

Height *Dog:* 25½–27¼ in (65–70cm) *Bitch:* 23½–25½ in (60–65cm)

Weight 73–77 lb (33–34.5kg)

Coat Hard, wiry, and very dense with a soft undercoat

Color Solid black or pepper and salt; all shades from dark iron-gray to silver-gray are acceptable; a small white spot on the breast is permissible

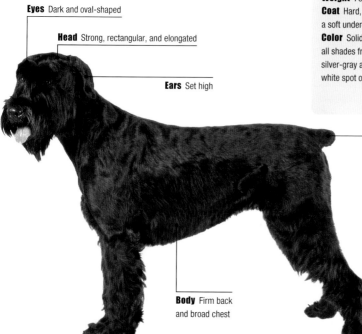

Eyes Dark and oval-shaped

Head Strong, rectangular, and elongated

Ears Set high

Tail Set and carried high, and characteristically docked to three joints

Body Firm back and broad chest

Miniature Schnauzer

Care requirements

1 2 3 4

1 2 3 4

1 2 3 4

1 2 3 4

Pedigree points

Recognized AKC, ANKC, CKC, FCI, KC(GB), KUSA

Height 12–14 in (30–35.5cm)

Weight 13–15 lb (6–7kg)

Coat Double, with a hard, wiry top coat and a close undercoat

Color Salt and pepper, black and silver, and solid black; all colors have uniform skin pigmentation

The Miniature Schnauzer was derived from crossing the Standard Schnauzer with smaller dogs (probably Affenpinschers). In the US and Canada, the Miniature Schnauzer is classed as a terrier and was at one time the most popular terrier there. In the UK, where it is regarded as a member of the utility group rather than a terrier, it is a popular family pet, and also does well in the obedience and show rings.

The Miniature Schnauzer is a delightful small dog that makes an excellent pet and children's companion. Like its larger contemporaries, it needs a fair amount of exercise and its coat should be periodically stripped and plucked. The coat may also be clipped but this will spoil it for the show ring, so it is best to discuss grooming with the breeder at the time of purchase.

Eyes Dark and oval-shaped

Head Strong and fairly long

Ears Set high

Tail Set and carried high, and characteristically docked to three joints

Body Short and deep with well-sprung ribcage

Schipperke

The Schipperke originated in Belgium but is often thought to be a Dutch dog, a confusion that may have arisen because the Netherlands and Belgium are relatively modern countries. The breed is thought by some to be 200 years old, although no records exist to prove this. It may have been established as long ago as the mid-1500s, because of a story that two black dogs without tails rescued Prince William of Orange from an assassin. Differences of opinion also exist on the breed's ancestry. Some think it arose from early northern spitz dogs, while others consider it a descendant of a now-extinct Belgian sheepdog.

The Schipperke was once the most popular housepet and watchdog in Belgium. Traditionally, its job was to guard canal barges when they were tied up for the night, and it was this task that earned the breed its name. Schipperke is Flemish for "little captain," and has also been translated as "little skipper," "little boatman," and even "little corporal."

This breed was first exhibited in 1880. It was recognized by the Royal Schipperke Club of Brussels in 1886, and given an official standard in 1904. The Schipperke Club of England was formed in 1905 and the Schipperke Club of America in 1929.

The Schipperke is an affectionate dog that is good with children, usually very long lived, and an excellent watchdog. It is said to be able to walk up to 6 miles (10km) a day without tiring, but will make do with considerably less exercise. It should be housed indoors rather than in a kennel, and its coat needs very little attention.

The Schipperke has a sharp, foxy expression and small, cat-like feet. Although other colors sometimes appear, it is generally pure black.

Head Broad with flat skull

Eyes Oval and dark brown

Ears Moderately long

Tail Docked

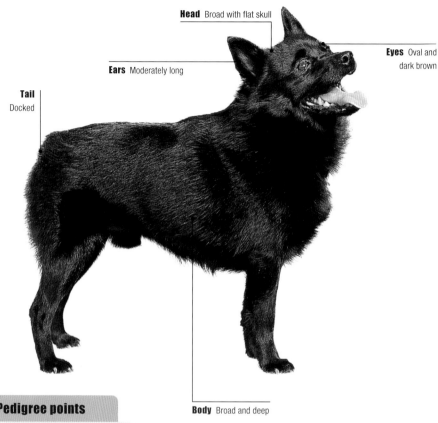

Body Broad and deep

Pedigree points

Recognized AKC, ANKC, CKC, FCI, KC(GB), KUSA
Height *Dog:* 11–13 in (27.5–32.5cm)
Bitch: 10–12 in (25–30cm)
Weight 12–18 lb (5.5–8kg)
Coat Abundant and dense, with longer hair on the neck, shoulders, chest, and backs of rear legs
Color Black, but the undercoat can be slightly lighter; other solid colors are permissible outside the US

Care requirements

	1	2	3	4
	1	2	3	4
	1	2	3	4
	1	2	3	4

Keeshond

The Keeshond (pronounced "kayshond," plural Keeshunden) has been known as the Fik, Foxdog, Dutch Barge Dog, and even as the Overweight Pomeranian in Victorian England. Its modern name is after a dog of this breed owned by the 18th-century Dutchman, Kees de Gyselaer. Like other spitz breeds, the Keeshond is believed to derive from an Arctic breed. It became popular in Holland as the companion of bargees and as a watchdog. The FCI has been reluctant to accept the standard that has been drawn up for the breed, believing that the Keeshond is identical to the German Wolfspitz.

Good natured and long lived, the Keeshond tends to be a devoted one-person dog. It requires daily grooming using a stiff brush, and a fair amount of exercise. A choke chain will spoil the ruff.

Care requirements

4   3   2   1

4   3   2   1

4   3   2   1

4   3   2   1

Pedigree points

Recognized AKC, ANKC, CKC, KC(GB), KUSA
Height *Dog:* 18 in (45.5cm)
Bitch: 17 in (43cm)
Weight 55–66 lb (25–29.5kg)
Coat Long and straight with the hairs standing out; a dense ruff over the neck
Color A mixture of gray, black, and cream; pale undercoat

Eyes Dark and medium-sized

Head Well-proportioned and wedge-shaped when seen from above

Ears Small and triangular

Tail Set high, well-feathered, and curling tightly over the back

Body Compact

Finnish Spitz

The Finnish Spitz is known in its native land as Suomenpystykorva, which means "cock-eared dog." It is the national dog of Finland, and is mentioned in a number of heroic Finnish national songs. It was once used by Lapp hunters to track elk and polar bears, but is now popular throughout Scandinavia for hunting grouse and other game birds. Related to the Russian Laika, the breed originated in the eastern area of Finland. It was introduced to and pioneered in Britain in the 1920s by the late Lady Kitty Ritson, who is responsible for the breed's nickname of Finkie.

While still a favorite with hunters in Scandinavia, the Finnish Spitz is kept almost entirely as a companion and show dog elsewhere. It is appreciated as a faithful and home-loving pet that is good with children and adept at guarding. It requires plenty of exercise and daily brushing.

Care requirements

1 2 3 4

1 2 3 4

1 2 3 4

1 2 3 4

Pedigree points

Recognized AKC, CKC, FCI, KC(GB)
Height *Dog:* 17–20 in (43–50cm)
Bitch: 15–18 in (39–45cm)
Weight 25–35 lb (11.5–16kg)
Coat Short and close on head and front of legs, longer on body and back of legs, semi-erect and stiff on neck and back
Color Reddish-brown or red-gold on back, preferably bright; lighter shades permissible on the underside

Head Medium-sized

Ears Small, cocked, and sharply pointed

Eyes Medium-sized

Tail Plumed and curving vigorously from the root

Body Almost square in outline

German Spitz

The only difference between the Small German Spitz and Standard German Spitz is size. Both are smaller versions of the Great German Spitz or Wolfspitz. Although it is difficult to pinpoint the origin of spitz dogs, they probably come from Scandinavia and were taken to other countries by the Vikings. Spitz dogs were known as early as 1700 when white specimens were said to be kept in Pomerania and black ones in Württemberg. Some of the smaller varieties of the white spitz bred in Pomerania became known and established under the name Pomeranian.

This active, intelligent dog is independent, yet devotion to its human family is a breed characteristic. The German Spitz can adapt to life in the town or country, and needs vigorous daily brushing and an average amount of exercise. If unchecked, the breed does have a tendency to yap.

Care requirements

4   3   2   1

4   3   2   1

4   3   2   1

4   3   2   1

Pedigree points

Recognized ANKC, FCI, KC(GB), KUSA
Height *Small:* 9–11 in (23–28cm)
Standard: 11½–13 in (29–35.5cm)
Weight *Small:* 7 lb (3kg)
Standard: 25 lb (11.5kg)
Coat Soft, woolly undercoat and long, dense, straight outer coat
Color All solid color varieties

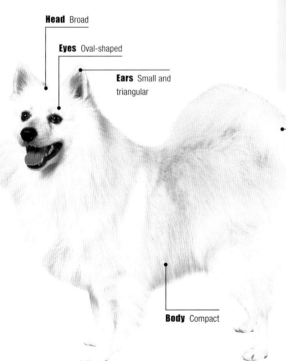

Head Broad

Eyes Oval-shaped

Ears Small and triangular

Tail Set high and carried curled over the body

Body Compact

Japanese Spitz

Care requirements

1 **2** 3 4

1 **2** 3 4

1 **2** 3 4

1 **2** 3 4

Pedigree points

Recognized ANKC, CKC, FCI, KC(GB), KUSA

Height *Dog:* 12–14 in (30–36cm)
Bitch: slightly smaller

Weight 13 lb (6kg)

Coat Straight, dense, stand-off outer coat; thick, short, dense undercoat

Color Pure white

The Japanese Spitz shares a common ancestry with the Nordic Spitz. It is about half the size of the Samoyed, and is also closely related to the German Spitz and Pomeranian. Its ancestors are said to have been taken to Japan in the ships of traders many years ago, and there the breed was developed in isolation. The breed is a family favorite in Japan. It has only recently become known internationally, and is proving a popular show dog.

The Japanese Spitz is a beautiful alert, intelligent, lively, and bold dog. Loyal to its owners but distrustful of strangers, it makes a fine small guard. The breed requires daily brushing, and having an instinctive desire to herd other animals, enjoys a fair amount of exercise.

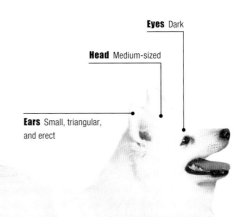

Eyes Dark

Head Medium-sized

Ears Small, triangular, and erect

Tail Set high and carried curled over back

Body Broad and deep

Chow Chow

The Chow Chow is the only dog with a black tongue, a characteristic it shares with some small bears. This lion-like member of the spitz family has been known in its native China for more than 2,000 years. It was bred variously for its flesh, its fur, and as a hunter of game, its name possibly deriving from the Chinese Choo Hunting Dog. The Chow Chow is said to have been the original "Mastiff" of the Tibetan Lama, and is also referred to in early Chinese writings as the Tartar Dog and the Dog of the Barbarians.

A former hunter of wolves, today the Chow Chow is a successful show dog and companion, as well as a good guard.

The first Chow Chow imported into Britain in 1760 was exhibited in a zoo. In 1895, the Chow Chow Club was formed there, and in 1905 the first member of the breed was exported from Britain to America. This was Mrs Garnett Botfield's Chinese Chum that, in 1905, became the first American Chow Chow champion. In 1936, Mrs V.A. Mawnooch's Champion Choonam Hung Kwong won the Best in Show title at Crufts Dog Show. He was the recipient of 44 British Challenge certificates and was valued at the then immense sum of £5,250 (US$8,400).

The Chow Chow has always had a reputation for ferocity, but although a formidable opponent, it is unlikely to attack unless provoked. It is a faithful, odor-free dog that makes a good pet, but prefers to look to one person as its master and needs firm but gentle handling. A good daily walk will suffice, but the full coat requires considerable attention with a wire brush.

Eyes Dark and almond-shaped

Head Broad and flat

Ears Small and slightly rounded at tips

Tail Set high and carried curled over the back

Body Compact with broad, deep chest

Pedigree points

Recognized AKC, ANKC, CKC, FCI, KC(GB), KUSA
Height *Dog:* 19–22 in (48–56cm)
Bitch: 18–20 in (46–51cm)
Weight 45–70 lb (20–31.5kg)
Coat Rough, abundant, dense, and coarse, with pronounced ruff around head and neck, and feathering on tail; or smooth, dense, and hard, with no ruff or feathering
Color Solid black, red, blue, fawn, or cream; blue-black tongue

Care requirements

	1	2	3	4
	1	2	3	4
	1	2	3	4
	1	2	3	4

Shiba Inu

The Shiba Inu is an ancient breed associated with the prefectures of Gifu, Toyama, and Nagano in central Japan, and the name, in fact, means "little dog" in the Nagano dialect. Remains of a dog of this type were found in ruins dating back to the Joman era (500 BC). The Shiba Inu has, in recent years, become a firm favorite of exhibitors, following closely on the heels of the Japanese Akita onto the international scene. It is an excellent bird dog, guard, and hunter of small game, with a considerable amount of native cunning.

The Shiba is an affectionate, friendly, and sensitive dog that makes a fine pet as well as a show dog and/or hunter. It needs a fair amount of exercise and a good daily brushing to keep it looking trim.

Care requirements

Pedigree points

Recognized ANKC, FCI, KC(GB)
Height *Dog:* 15–16 in (37.5–40cm)
Bitch: 14–15 in (35–37.5cm)
Weight 20–30 lb (9–13.5kg)
Coat Harsh and straight
Color Red, salt and pepper, black, black and tan, or white

Eyes Almond-shaped

Ears Small, triangular, and firmly pricked

Head Broad, flat forehead

Tail Long and sickle-shaped

Body Sturdily built and well-muscled, with deep chest and long back

Shar-Pei

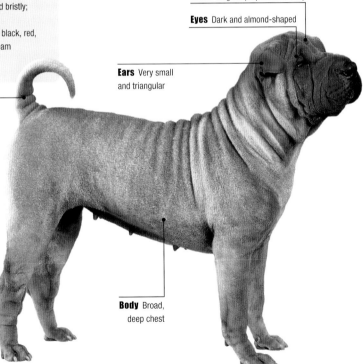
There are likenesses of the Shar-Pei or Chinese Fighting Dog dating back to the Han Dynasty (206 BC–AD 220), and it has been suggested that this loose-skinned breed may have originated in Tibet or China's Northern Province some 2,000 years ago. The Shar-Pei was used to herd flocks and hunt wild boar in China, and was also matched against other dogs in trials of strength, although its nature is so affable that it may have had to be provoked to do so with the aid of drugs. It is not long since the Shar-Pei had the distinction of being the rarest dog in the world, but now it is drawing good entries in the show ring.

A very affectionate dog with a frowning expression, the Shar-Pei is calm, independent, and devoted. Its coat is never trimmed, and it needs a reasonable amount of exercise.

Care requirements

1 2 3 4

1 2 3 4

1 2 3 4

1 2 3 4

Pedigree points

Recognized AKC, ANKC, FCI, KC(GB), KUSA
Height 18–20 in (46–51cm)
Weight 40–55 lb (18–25kg)
Coat Short, straight, and bristly; no undercoat
Color Solid colors only: black, red, light or dark fawn, or cream

Head Large in proportion to body

Eyes Dark and almond-shaped

Ears Very small and triangular

Tail Rounded, narrowing to a fine point, set high, and curling over to either side of the back

Body Broad, deep chest

Shih Tzu

The Shih Tzu, whose Chinese name means "lion dog," is generally thought to have originated in western China. It resembles a Lhasa Apso except for its shortened face, and could be the result of crossing the Lhasa Apso and the Pekingese. Certainly it was the practice of the Dalai Lama of Tibet to give prize specimens of the Lhasa Apso to visiting dignitaries from foreign lands, including those from China. An early standard for the breed written by the Peking Kennel Club, called the most flowery ever issued, reads: "should have lion head, bear torso, camel hoof, feather-duster tail, palm-leaf ears, rice teeth, pearly petal tongue, and movement like a goldfish."

This happy, hardy little dog loves children and other animals and makes a good housepet suited to town or country living. It requires a good daily grooming using a bristle brush, and the topknot is usually tied with a bow.

Care requirements

4	3	2	1
4	3	2	1
4	3	2	1
4	3	2	1

Pedigree points

Recognized AKC, ANKC, CKC, FCI, KC(GB), KUSA

Height 9–10½ in (22.5–26.5cm)

Weight 9–18 lb (4–8kg)

Coat Long, dense, not curly, with a good undercoat

Color All colors permissible; white blaze on forehead and white tip on tail highly desirable in particolors

Eyes Large, dark, and round

Head Broad, round, and wide between the eyes

Ears Large, with long feathers, and carried drooping

Tail Heavily plumed and carried curved well over the back

Body Longer between withers and root of tail than height at withers

Lhasa Apso

Pedigree points

Recognized AKC, ANKC, CKC, FCI, KC(GB), KUSA

Height *Dog:* 10 in (25.5cm)
Bitch: slightly smaller

Coat Top coat long, heavy, straight, and hard, not woolly or silky; moderate undercoat

Color Solid golden, sandy, honey, dark grizzle, slate, or smoke; black particolor, white, or brown

The Lhasa Apso originated in Tibet and is sometimes known as the Tibetan Apso. It is a small, indoor watchdog, possibly bred in the distant past from the Tibetan Mastiff. The word apso means goat-like, and the dog may have been so named because its coat resembled that of the goats kept by Tibetan herders. The breed was very highly regarded in its native land, and kept in temples and palaces. The Lhasa is often confused with the Shih Tzu from western China, but there are a number of physical differences between them, including the fact that the Lhasa Apso has a longer nose and its nose-tip is placed lower. However, in the past there seems to have been some interbreeding between them outside their native lands.

The Lhasa Apso is happy, usually long lived, adaptable, and good with children. It enjoys a good romp outdoors, but it does require careful daily grooming of its long coat.

Ears Heavily feathered

Head Long hair covering eyes and reaching toward floor

Eyes Dark

Tail Set high and carried over the back

Body Compact and well-balanced

Non-sporting Breeds

Tibetan Spaniel

Despite its name, this breed is not related to the spaniels and is not known to have been used as a hunting companion or gundog. The Tibetan Spaniel is thought to have been in existence long before the history of Tibet started to be chronicled in the 7th century, and its origins are therefore obscure. The exchange of dogs between Tibet and China in ancient times means that Chinese dogs, such as early Shih Tzu or Pekingese-like dogs, could have contributed to it. It has also been said that the Tibetan Spaniel was crossed with the Pug to bring about the Pekingese. The Tibetan Spaniel was a favorite with monks, and it is said that it turned the prayer wheel of Tibetans. It is also said that it was used by humans for warmth.

This charming, good-natured dog is rarely seen outside the show ring. It is intelligent, good with children, and makes a splendid housepet. It is energetic and enjoys a good romp, and its coat needs regular grooming.

Care requirements

4   3   2   1

4   3   2   1

4   3   2   1

4   3   2   1

Pedigree points

Recognized AKC, ANKC, CKC, FCI, KC(GB), KUSA
Height 10 in (25.5cm)
Weight 9–15 lb (4–7kg)
Coat Moderately long and silky in texture; shorter on face and fronts of legs; feathering on ears, backs of legs, and tail
Color All solid colors and mixtures

Head Small in proportion to body

Eyes Dark brown and expressive

Ears Medium-sized and pendant

Tail Set high, richly plumed, and carried curled over the back

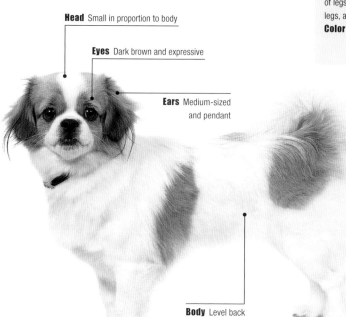

Body Level back with good depth

Tibetan Terrier

The Tibetan Terrier is not really a terrier at all, having no history of going to earth, but resembles a small Old English Sheepdog. Like other little Tibetan dogs, it appears not to have been bred for any purpose other than that of companion dog. Of ancient lineage, the Tibetan Terrier is said to have been bred in Tibetan monasteries, and specimens used to be presented to travelers as mascots and to bring luck. The breed was included in the Tibetan Breeds Association register in 1934 and now has its own standard.

The Tibetan Terrier might prove the ideal pet for those who admire the Old English Sheepdog but cannot house such a large animal. This appealing, shaggy little dog is also worth choosing for its own sake. It is loyal, sturdy, a good walker, and devoted to its owners and to children, but a little apprehensive of strangers. Its long coat needs regular attention.

Head Medium and well-furnished with long hair

Eyes Large, round, and dark

Ears Pendant and feathered

Tail Set quite high and carried curled over the back

Body Compact and powerful

Bichon Frise

The word bichon is often used collectively to describe small, white dogs. The Bichon Frise or Bichon à Poil Frise (curly-haired bichon), or Tenerife Dog, is reputed to have been introduced to Tenerife in the Canary Islands by sailors in the 14th century. However, like the Poodle, it is thought to be a descendant of the French water dog, the Barbet, and its name comes from the diminutive, *barbichon*. Similar in appearance to the Miniature Poodle, the Bichon Frise is recognized internationally as a Franco-Belgian breed.

Happy, friendly, and lively, this breed makes an attractive and cuddly small pet that will enjoy as much exercise as most owners can provide. However, its long curly coat, resembling a powder puff, means that it is not the choice for anyone averse to grooming. The scissoring and trimming required to achieve this shape is intricate, and anyone intending to exhibit should discuss what is entailed with the breeder at the time of purchase.

Care requirements

4	3	2	1
4	3	2	1
4	3	2	1
4	3	2	1

Pedigree points

Recognized AKC, ANKC, CKC, FCI, KC(GB), KUSA
Height 9–11 in (23–28cm)
Coat Long and loosely curling
Color White, cream, or apricot markings permissible up to 18 months; dark skin desirable

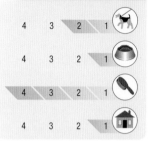

Head Slightly rounded on a relatively long, arched neck

Ears Long and hanging close to head

Eyes Dark and round with black rims

Tail Carried gracefully curved over the body

Body Wide, well-developed chest and level topline

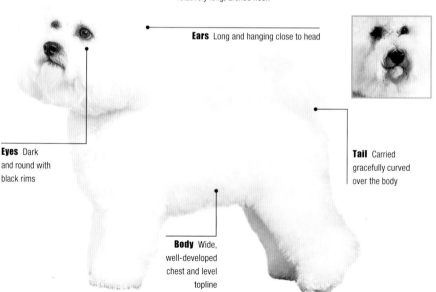

Standard Poodle

Care requirements

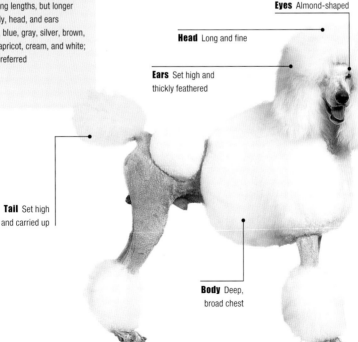

1 2 **3** 4

1 **2** 3 4

1 2 **3** 4

1 **2** 3 4

Pedigree points

Recognized AKC, ANKC, CKC, FCI, KC(GB), KUSA
Height Over 15 in (38cm)
Weight 45–70 lb (20–31.5kg)
Coat *Curly:* harsh texture and dense throughout *Corded:* hanging in tight cords of varying lengths, but longer on mane, body, head, and ears
Color Black, blue, gray, silver, brown, café-au-lait, apricot, cream, and white; clear colors preferred

Known in France as the Caniche, the Poodle was certainly favored by the French Queen Marie Antoinette. However, it originated in Germany as a water retriever, or Pudel in German. It resembles the Irish Water Spaniel, and both share common ancestors in the French Barbet. The Standard Poodle still retains its ability as a gundog and swims well. Its intelligence and eagerness to learn mean that it is popular in obedience trials and as a circus dog.

This happy, lively dog makes a good pet, enjoying a fair amount of exercise. It is also a fine show dog, provided you have the time for intricate preparation. While it is shown in the lion clip, many pet owners prefer the lamb clip (with hair uniform length). Whatever style you choose, you will need to use a wire-pin pneumatic brush and a wire-toothed metal comb for daily grooming. Even the pet Poodle must attend the canine beauty parlor every six weeks or so.

Eyes Almond-shaped

Head Long and fine

Ears Set high and thickly feathered

Tail Set high and carried up

Body Deep, broad chest

Miniature Poodle

The Miniature Poodle was bred down from the Standard, presumably by using the smaller specimens. During the 1950s, it became the most popular breed in many countries because it was believed, wrongly, that as more people migrated to the towns, interest in working breeds would lessen. While there are those who say that it is not a proper dog at all—unaware of its origins as a gundog and water retriever, no doubt—the Miniature Poodle remains a favorite.

The Miniature Poodle has the same show standard as the larger and smaller breeds, except in the matter of size, and has similar characteristics. It requires frequent regular visits to the canine beauty parlor, even if it is not the intention to exhibit. Use a wire-pin pneumatic brush and a wire-toothed metal comb for daily grooming.

Care requirements

4	3	2	1	
4	3	2	1	
4	3	2	1	
4	3	2	1	

Pedigree points

Recognized AKC, ANKC, CKC, FCI, KC(GB), KUSA
Height 10–15 in (25–37.5cm)
Coat Naturally harsh, and can be curly or corded
Color All solid colors; clear colors preferred

Head Long with flat cheekbones

Ears Set high and hanging close to chest

Eyes Dark amber or dark brown

Tail Set high and carried up

Body Deep, broad, strongly muscled chest

Toy Poodle

Pedigree points

Recognized AKC, ANKC, CKC, FCI, KC(GB), KUSA

Height Under 10 in (25cm)

Coat Very profuse and dense with a good, harsh texture; curly or corded

Color All solid colors; brown and café-au-lait have liver noses, eye rims, and lips; all others have black noses, eye rims, and lips

The Toy Poodle is a descendant of the Miniature Poodle. The smaller specimens were so much in demand that, by the middle of the 1950s, the UK Kennel Club agreed to open a separate register for them. These are the least robust of the three varieties, however, so it is essential to select from sound stock.

The Toy Poodle has the same characteristics and show standard as its larger counterparts, except in the matter of size. It is happy and good tempered and makes a delightful pet that is ideal for the apartment dweller who nonetheless enjoys a canine companion. The Toy is exhibited in the same clips as the other two varieties. In any case, it will require regular visits to the canine beauty parlor. Use a wire-pin pneumatic brush and a wire-toothed metal comb for daily grooming.

Eyes Almond-shaped and set far apart

Head Long and fine

Tail Set high and carried up

Body Well-sprung ribcage

Ears Set high and hanging close to chest

Working Breeds

Working Breeds

Mastiff

The Mastiff is among the most ancient breeds of dog and has proved its worth as a formidable guard and hunter. Mastiff-like dogs were treasured by the Babylonians over 4,000 years ago, and when Julius Caesar invaded Britain in 55 BC, he encountered Mastiffs fighting alongside their masters. He subsequently sent some back to Rome, where they fought in the huge arenas and defeated all other fighting dogs, as well as being matched against gladiators, bulls, bears, lions, and tigers. The Mastiff was depicted on the 12th-century Bayeux Tapestry, and Shakespeare's play *Henry V* mentions "mastiffs of unmatchable courage." In the 19th century, Saint Bernard blood was introduced.

The Mastiff is large and dignified. It is usually devoted to its owner and needs regular walking to build up its muscles. Many do not complete growth until their second year.

Care requirements

4	3	2	1
4	3	2	1
4	3	2	1
4	3	2	1

Pedigree points

Recognized AKC, ANKC, CKC, FCI, KC(GB), KUSA
Height *Dog:* 30 in (75cm)
Bitch: 27½ in (68.5cm)
Weight 175–190 lb (78.5–85.5kg)
Coat Outer coat short and straight; undercoat dense and close
Color Apricot, fawn, or brindle; in all, the muzzle, ears, and nose should be black, with black around the eyes and extending up between them

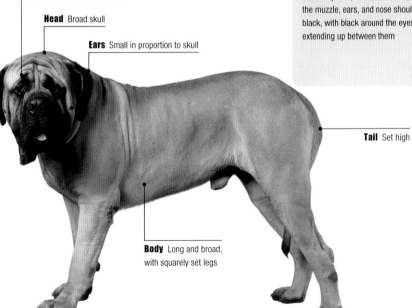

Eyes Small and set wide apart

Head Broad skull

Ears Small in proportion to skull

Tail Set high

Body Long and broad, with squarely set legs

Tibetan Mastiff

Care requirements

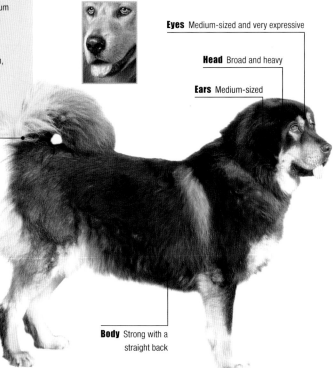

1 2 3 4

1 2 3 4

1 2 3 4

1 2 3 4

Pedigree points

Recognized ANKC, FCI, KC(GB), KUSA

Height *Dog:* 26 in (66cm) minimum
Bitch: 24 in (61cm) minimum

Weight 180 lb (81.5kg) minimum

Coat Medium length, thicker on males than females, with a heavy undercoat

Color Rich black, black and tan, brown, various shades of gold, various shades of gray, or gray with gold markings

The Tibetan Mastiff is one of many breeds descended from the Molossus, a fighting dog of ancient Rome. It originated in central Asia, where it guarded flocks, and it can still be found in the central Asian steppes and around the Himalayan foothills performing the same task for nomadic shepherds. There is mention of the Tibetan Mastiff in the 13th-century chronicles of the explorer Marco Polo, who referred to native mastiffs "as large as asses." This was possibly an exaggeration, but it is certainly an imposing dog.

This breed makes a fine companion, watchdog, and guard. It is aloof, protective, and slow to mature, reaching its best at 2–3 years in females and at least 4 years in males. The Tibetan Mastiff has a reliable temperament unless provoked, and needs regular vigorous exercise on hard ground and daily brushing.

Eyes Medium-sized and very expressive

Head Broad and heavy

Ears Medium-sized

Tail Medium to long

Body Strong with a straight back

Working Breeds

Bullmastiff

There have been bulldogs in Britain since the 13th century, but the Bullmastiff was developed some 200–300 years ago. It is the result of a cross between the Mastiff, an ancient breed that fought in the arenas of ancient Rome, and the British Bulldog. Like the Bulldog, it was used in bull-baiting until this "sport" was outlawed, and was a brave fighting dog that could bear pain without flinching. It also had a considerable reputation for ferocity. Later breeders worked toward a type that was 60 percent Mastiff and 40 percent Bulldog.

Despite its ferocious past, the Bullmastiff of today is a playful, loyal, and gentle animal, an excellent guard, and usually very dependable with children. However, it is too powerful for a child or slight adult to control, and should only be kept by experienced dog owners. It needs grooming every few days.

Care requirements

4	3	2	1	
4	3	2	1	
4	3	2	1	
4	3	2	1	

Pedigree points

Recognized AKC, ANKC, CKC, FCI, KC(GB), KUSA
Height *Dog:* 25–27 in (63.5–68.5cm)
Bitch: 24–26 in (61–66cm)
Weight *Dog:* 110–130 lb (50–59kg)
Bitch: 90–110 lb (41–50kg)
Coat Short, smooth, and dense
Color Any shade of brindle, fawn, or red; slight white marking on the chest is permissible, other white markings are undesirable; black muzzle

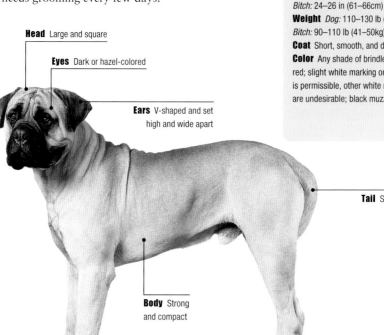

Head Large and square

Eyes Dark or hazel-colored

Ears V-shaped and set high and wide apart

Tail Set high

Body Strong and compact

Great Dane

Care requirements

Pedigree points

Recognized AKC, ANKC, CKC, FCI, KC(GB), KUSA
Height Minimum over 18 months
Dog: 30 in (76cm) *Bitch:* 28 in (71cm)
Weight Minimum over 18 months
Dog: 120 lb (54kg) *Bitch:* 100 lb (46kg)
Coat Short, dense, and sleek
Color Brindle, fawn, blue, black, or harlequin (white, preferably with all black or all blue patches that have the appearance of being torn)

The Great Dane is known in its native Germany as the German Mastiff. This statuesque dog, often referred to as the Apollo of the dog world, is said to be descended from the Molossus hounds of ancient Rome. In the Middle Ages, it was used as a wild boar hunter, companion, and bodyguard, and the breed also played its part in bull-baiting. In the 1800s, the Chancellor of Germany, Bismarck, who had a particular interest in mastiffs, crossed the mastiff of southern Germany and the Great Dane of the north to produce dogs similar to the Dane we know today.

Despite its size, this breed should not be kenneled outdoors, but kept indoors as a member of the family. The Great Dane is good natured, playful, and easy to train. However, it should not be teased lest an action be misinterpreted. It needs regular exercise on hard ground and daily grooming with a body brush. It lives for only 8–9 years on average.

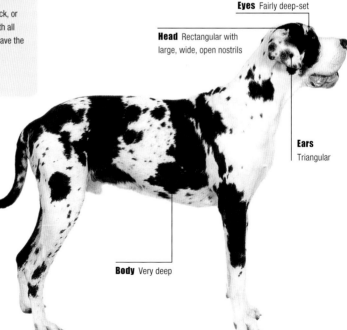

Eyes Fairly deep-set
Head Rectangular with large, wide, open nostrils
Tail Thick at the root and tapering toward the tip
Ears Triangular
Body Very deep

Boxer

The Boxer traces back to the mastiff-type dogs taken into battle against the Romans by the Cimbrians, a Germanic tribe. The breed was first exhibited in Munich in 1895, and a Boxer was registered by the American Kennel Club as early as 1904. However, it was not until after World War I that the Boxer began to attain its immense popularity worldwide.

The Boxer is an affectionate, playful breed that retains its puppyish ways well into maturity and is usually good with children. This obedient and loyal dog also makes a good guard. It is, however, very strong and is not averse to fighting with its fellows. It needs a reasonable amount of exercise, and its short coat is easy to care for.

Care requirements

4	3	2	1
4	3	2	1
4	3	2	1
4	3	2	1

Pedigree points

Recognized AKC, ANKC, CKC, FCI, KC(GB), KUSA
Height *Dog:* 22½–25 in (57–63cm)
Bitch: 21–23 in (53–59cm)
Weight 53–71 lb (24–32kg)
Coat Short, glossy, and smooth
Color Fawn or brindle with any white markings not exceeding one third of ground color

Eyes Dark brown and forward-looking

Head Slightly arched skull with flat cheeks

Ears Moderate-sized and set wide apart

Tail Set high and characteristically docked

Body Square in profile with well-defined chest

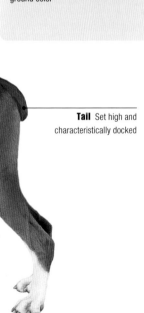

Care requirements

	1	2	3	4
1	2	3	4
1	2	3	4
1	2	3	4

Pedigree points

Recognized AKC, ANKC, CKC, FCI, KC(GB), KUSA

Height *Dog:* 26–28 in (65–70cm)
Bitch: 24–26 in (60–65cm)

Weight 66–88 lb (29.5–39.5kg)

Coat Smooth, short, thick, and close

Color Solid black, brown, blue, or fawn, with rust markings on head, body, and legs

Doberman

The Doberman was developed in the 1880s by Louis Doberman of Apolda in Germany. He wanted a ferocious, short-coated, medium- to large-sized dog with courage and stamina, and developed his stock around the German Pinscher, which was both alert and aggressive. To this he introduced the Rottweiler with its stamina and tracking ability, the Manchester Terrier from which the Doberman inherited its markings, and possibly also the Pointer. The Doberman was given official recognition as a breed standard in Germany in 1900.

A fine obedience and show dog, the Doberman can make a good family pet, but it needs knowledgeable handling and training, being wary of strangers and constantly "on guard." It needs a lot of exercise, and should be groomed every couple of days.

Eyes Almond-shaped

Head Long with flat skull on well-arched neck

Ears Small, neat, and set high on head

Tail Characteristically docked at second joint

Body Square and muscular

Komondor

The Komondor was known as early as 1555, and has been used for centuries to guard flocks and property from predators and thieves on the Hungarian plains. Very strong and agile for its size, the Komondor is hardy, healthy, and tolerant of changing temperatures. It is a breed that can never be mistaken for any other because of its full white coat falling in tassels, or cords, which form a kind of controlled matting that feels felty to the touch.

The Komondor is a natural protector and will guard children and other pets with its life if it is cast in the role of family companion. While it is utterly devoted to its human family, it is wary of strangers, does not take kindly to teasing, and if a warning growl goes unheeded, may attack without warning. It needs plenty of exercise and meticulous grooming.

Care requirements

4	3	2	1	🐕
4	3	2	1	🥣
4	3	2	1	🪮
4	3	2	1	🏠

Pedigree points

Recognized AKC, ANKC, CKC, FCI, KC(GB), KUSA
Height *Dog:* 25 in (63.5cm)
Bitch: 23½ in (58.5cm)
Weight 80–150 lb (36.5–68kg)
Coat Long, coarse outer coat; may be curly or wavy; softer undercoat
Color White

Eyes Medium-sized

Head Short in relation to its width, on muscular, slightly arched neck

Ears Medium-sized

Tail Long, continuing line of rump, and slightly curved at tip

Body
Level back

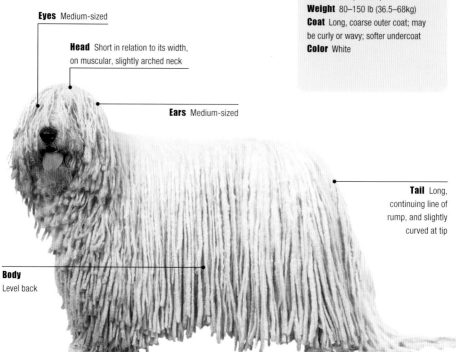

Canaan Dog

The Canaan Dog is an indigenous breed of Israel that is said to have been developed through the selective breeding of the semi-wild Pariah dogs of the Middle East. A fine guard and protector of livestock, the Canaan has also proved its worth as a guard dog and as a messenger in the Israeli army. Other uses have been as a guide dog for the blind and as a search and rescue dog. There are two varieties of Canaan Dog, one collie-like and the other Dingo-like, the latter being more heavily built.

The Canaan is alert, home loving, and loyal to its family. It has a distrust of strangers and will faithfully guard the humans and animals entrusted to its care, standing its ground if called upon to do so. It needs regular grooming with a brush and comb.

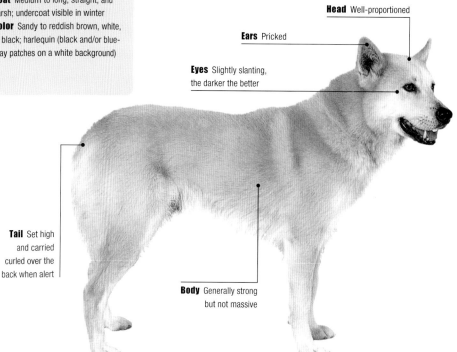

Head Well-proportioned

Ears Pricked

Eyes Slightly slanting, the darker the better

Tail Set high and carried curled over the back when alert

Body Generally strong but not massive

Rottweiler

In its native Germany, this breed is still referred to as the Rottweiler Metzgerhund (Rottweil Butcher's Dog), because in the past it worked as a draft dog delivering meat. It has also been used as a hunter of wild boar and a trusted cattle dog. Some fanciers believe that the Rottweiler is a descendant of the early German Shepherd Dog, while others consider that its ancestor was similar to the Tibetan Mastiff, brought as a guard by Roman soldiers. During World War I, it proved itself to be an intelligent police dog and guard.

The Rottweiler is a large, courageous dog that makes an excellent companion/guard and responds to kind but firm handling. However, an inexperienced owner should never keep this breed, nor should anyone who does not have considerable time to devote to its training. It needs space and plenty of exercise, and daily grooming with a bristle brush or hound glove and comb.

Care requirements

Pedigree points

Recognized AKC, ANKC, CKC, FCI, KC(GB), KUSA
Height *Dog:* 24–27 in (60–69cm)
Bitch: 22–25 in (55–63.5cm)
Weight 90–110 lb (40.5–48.5kg)
Coat Medium length, coarse, and flat, with undercoat on neck and thighs
Color Black with clearly defined tan or deep brown markings

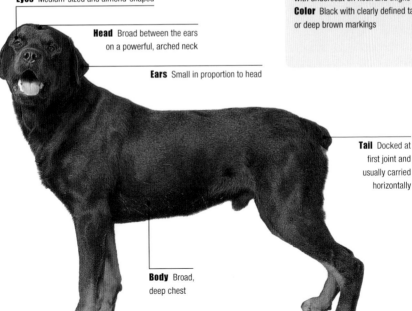

Eyes Medium-sized and almond-shaped

Head Broad between the ears on a powerful, arched neck

Ears Small in proportion to head

Tail Docked at first joint and usually carried horizontally

Body Broad, deep chest

Leonberger

Care requirements

	1	2	3	4
🐕	1	2	3	4
🍲	1	2	3	4
🖌	1	2	3	4
🏠	1	2	3	4

Pedigree points

Recognized ANKC, CKC, FCI, KC(GB), KUSA
Height *Dog:* 28–32 in (72–80cm)
Bitch: 26–30 in (65–75cm)
Weight 80–150 lb (36.5–68kg)
Coat Medium soft, fairly long, and close to body
Color Light yellow, or golden to red-brown; preferably with black mask

A German breed, the Leonberger is generally thought to have come about through the crossing of a Landseer and a Pyrenean Mountain Dog. However, some people believe that it is a descendant of the Tibetan Mastiff, while others consider it to be the product of selective breeding by Herr Essig of Leonberg. He is said to have used the Newfoundland, Saint Bernard, and Pyrenean Mountain Dog to develop the breed. The breed was devastated by both World Wars and is considered a rare breed.

Good natured, intelligent, and lively, the Leonberger is a fine-looking watchdog, produced from breeds of sound temperament. It is essentially a country dog, and needs daily brushing, regular exercise, and plenty of space. It is very good with children, and has a great love of water.

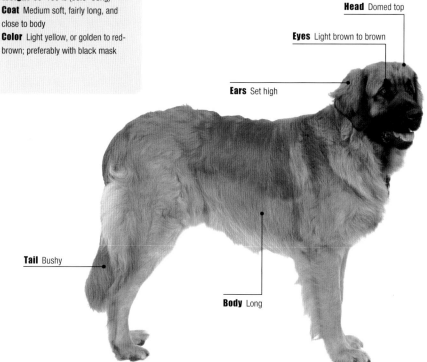

Head Domed top

Eyes Light brown to brown

Ears Set high

Tail Bushy

Body Long

Portuguese Water Dog

The Portuguese Water Dog was once a familiar sight throughout the fishing ports of the Iberian Peninsula, and is still commonly found in the Algarve region of Portugal. It is a fisherman's dog and undertakes a wide variety of tasks, including guarding the catch and retrieving fish or objects lost overboard. There are two distinct varieties of the breed, one with a long, glossy, wavy coat and the other with a shorter, thicker, curlier coat, but conformation is identical.

This intelligent, energetic dog is self-willed but obedient to its owner, and somewhat apprehensive of strangers. It is a superlative swimmer and diver, needs ample exercise, and regular brushing and combing. For exhibition, the hindquarters are clipped from the last rib, and two-thirds of the tail are clipped.

Care requirements

4	3	2	1	
4	3	2	1	
4	3	2	1	
4	3	2	1	

Pedigree points

Recognized AKC, ANKC, CKC, FCI, KC(GB), KUSA
Height *Dog:* 19½–23 in (50–57.5cm)
Bitch: 17–21 in (43–52.5cm)
Weight *Dog:* 42–60 lb (19–27kg)
Bitch: 35–50 lb (15.5–22.5kg)
Coat Profuse and thick except under forelegs and thighs; either fairly long and slightly waved or shortish and compact curls; no undercoat
Color Solid black, white, or various shades of brown; black and white or brown and white; skin bluish under black, white, and black and white

Ears Heart-shaped and dropped

Head Large and well-proportioned

Eyes Round and set well apart

Tail Thick at base and tapering toward point

Body Deep chest

Japanese Akita

Care requirements

🐕	1	2	3	4
🥣	1	2	3	4
🖌	1	2	3	4
🏠	1	2	3	4

Pedigree points

Recognized AKC, ANKC, CKC, FCI, KC(GB)

Height *Dog:* 26–28 in (66–71cm)
Bitch: 24–26 in (61–66cm)

Weight 75–101 lb (33.5–48.5kg)

Coat Outer coat coarse, straight, and stand-off; soft, dense undercoat

Color Any, including white, brindle, and pinto (white with irregular black patches), with or without mask

The Akita originated in the Polar regions and has a history tracing back more than 300 years. The Akita was bred to hunt deer and wild boar, and has also hunted the Japanese black bear. It is an extremely swift-moving dog that can work in deep snow. It also has webbed feet and is a strong swimmer, with the ability to retrieve wildfowl and to drive fish into fishermen's nets.

The powerful but very trainable Akita is a versatile hunter and retriever, and a first-class guard. It has a good temperament for a show dog and is now being kept widely as a pet. However, this alert and energetic dog should not be kept in confined conditions. It can be formidable if its hunting instincts become aroused and needs a good outlet, such as obedience classes, for its undoubted abilities. It also requires daily brushing and a reasonable amount of exercise.

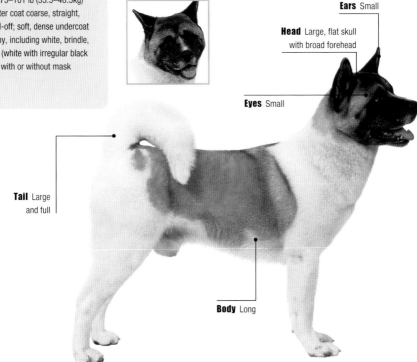

Ears Small

Head Large, flat skull with broad forehead

Eyes Small

Tail Large and full

Body Long

Estrela Mountain Dog

The Estrela Mountain Dog, also known as the Portuguese Mountain Dog, originated many centuries ago in the Estrêla mountains of Portugal. It was bred as a herding dog and has in its make-up something of the Mastiff and the Saint Bernard, to which it bears some resemblance. It has always been popular in its native Portugal, where it is still used as a guard dog.

The Estrela Mountain Dog is an excellent guard, with immense stamina. It is very loyal and affectionate to its owners but indifferent to other humans. This intelligent dog is said to need a great deal of love and firm, kind handling. It requires plenty of exercise, regular brushing, and a light diet, which should be discussed with the breeder at the time of purchase.

Care requirements

4   3   2   1

4   3   2   1

4   3   2   1

4   3   2   1

Pedigree points

Recognized FCI, KC(GB), KUSA
Height *Dog:* 23–27 in (58–68cm)
Bitch: 20–24 in (51–61cm)
Weight *Dog:* 75–105 lb (34–48kg)
Bitch: 60–90 lb (27–41kg)
Coat *Long:* thick, moderately harsh outer coat with feathering on backs of legs and thighs, and dense undercoat
Short: thick, moderately harsh outer coat, with shorter, dense undercoat
Color All colors or combinations of colors

Eyes Neither deep nor prominent

Head Long and powerful

Ears Small in proportion to body

Tail Long and thick

Body Short back, higher at withers than loins

Pyrenean Mountain Dog

The Pyrenean Mountain Dog or Great Pyrenees probably originated in Asia before finding its way with immigrants to Europe. Its closest relatives are the Kuvasz and the Newfoundland, to which it may have contributed. The breed has been used for centuries to guard flocks in the Pyrenean mountains bordering France and Spain, and throughout France.

The Pyrenean can be kept in or outdoors, but must be well trained. It is a powerful dog, but is generally good natured, gets on with other pets, and is a faithful protector. If you have sufficient space, food, and time for regular exercise and brushing, the Pyrenean will make a good companion and/or show dog.

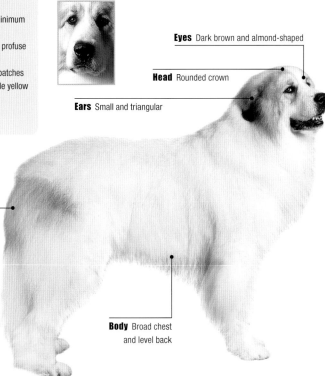

Eyes Dark brown and almond-shaped

Head Rounded crown

Ears Small and triangular

Tail Thick at root and tapering toward tip

Body Broad chest and level back

Bernese Mountain Dog

The Bernese Mountain Dog is named after the canton of Berne in Switzerland, where it arrived with the Roman army and was subsequently bred. Like other Swiss mountain dogs, it has mastiff characteristics. The breed is believed to descend from the Molossus dog of ancient Greece and Rome, with some Rottweiler, Saint Bernard, and Newfoundland blood discernible in its ancestry. The Bernese has worked as herder and flock guardian in its native land, and is still used to pull milk carts up Swiss mountainsides.

The Bernese Mountain Dog makes a good pet for those with sufficient space, being amiable toward children and other pets. It needs regular brushing and plenty of exercise.

Care requirements

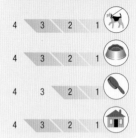

4	3	2	1	🐕
4	3	2	1	🥣
4	3	2	1	🖌
4	3	2	1	🏠

Pedigree points

Recognized AKC, ANKC, CKC, FCI, KC(GB), KUSA
Height *Dog:* 25–27½ in (64–70cm) *Bitch:* 23–26 in (58–66cm)
Weight 88 lb (39.5kg)
Coat Thick, moderately long, and straight or slightly wavy, with a bright, natural sheen
Color Jet black, with reddish brown markings on cheeks, eyes, legs, and chest; some white markings on head, chest, tail tip, and feet are permissible

Eyes Dark brown and almond-shaped

Head Strong with a flat skull

Ears Medium-sized

Tail Bushy

Body Compact

Care requirements

	1	2	3	4
	1	2	3	4
	1	2	3	4
	1	2	3	4

Pedigree points

Recognized AKC, ANKC, CKC, FCI, KC(GB), KUSA
Height *Dog:* 27½ in (69cm)
Bitch: 23½ in (64cm)
Weight 110–200 lb (48.5–90kg)
Coat Dense, short, smooth, and lying close to body
Color Orange, mahogany-brindle, red-brindle, or white, with patches on body in any of these colors; white blaze on face, and white on muzzle, collar, chest, forelegs, feet, and end of tail; black shadings on face and ears

Saint Bernard

The Saint Bernard is a gentle giant, despite being descended from the fierce Molossus dogs of ancient Rome. It is named after the medieval Hospice of St. Bernard in the Swiss Alps, where it became famous for rescuing travelers and climbers. Prior to 1830, all Saint Bernards were short-coated, but in that year Newfoundland blood was introduced in an attempt to give the breed added size and vitality. As a result, the modern Saint Bernard may be long- or short-haired.

True to its past, the Saint Bernard is intelligent, eminently trainable, loves children, and is a kindly dog. Like many heavyweights, the breed should not be given too much exercise in the first year of life, with short regular walks being better than long ones. It needs daily brushing and requires generous quantities of food. It also slobbers. Sadly, like the Great Dane, this lovable, large dog has only a limited lifespan.

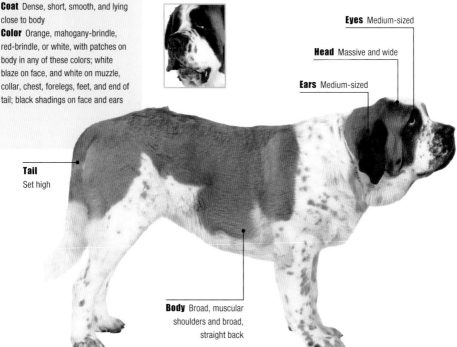

Eyes Medium-sized
Head Massive and wide
Ears Medium-sized
Tail Set high
Body Broad, muscular shoulders and broad, straight back

Working Breeds

Eskimo Dog

This hardy, strong spitz dog was developed to haul sleds in and around the Arctic Circle. The American polar explorer Robert Peary considered that there was only one breed of sled dog with regional variations, but now a number of breeds are recognized. The Eskimo Dog probably originated in eastern Siberia, and shared common ancestry with the Alaskan Malamute, Siberian Husky, and Samoyed. It bears a considerable resemblance to the Greenland Dog, but the Eskimo Dog is shorter in the back and weightier.

The Eskimo Dog is an excellent sled dog of remarkable endurance. It is a fine guard and rarely lives indoors with its owners. It relishes vigorous outdoor exercise and a job of work, and benefits from regular brushing.

Care requirements

Pedigree points

Recognized FCI, KC(GB), KUSA
Height *Dog:* 23–27 in (58–68cm)
Bitch: 20–24 in (51–61cm)
Weight *Dog:* 75–105 lb (33.5–47kg)
Bitch: 60–90 lb (27–40.5kg)
Coat About 6 in (15cm) long, with a thick undercoat
Color Any color or combination of colors

Eyes Dark brown or tawny

Head Well-proportioned

Ears Short, firm, and set well apart

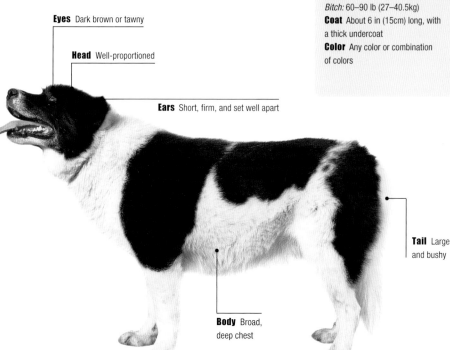

Tail Large and bushy

Body Broad, deep chest

Alaskan Malamute

1 2 3 4

1 2 3 4

1 2 3 4

1 2 3 4

Pedigree points

Recognized AKC, ANKC, CKC, FCI, KC(GB), KUSA

Height *Dog:* 25–28 in (64–71cm)
Bitch: 23–26 in (58–66cm)

Weight 85–125 lb (38.5–57kg)

Coat Thick, coarse guard coat; dense, oily, woolly undercoat

Color From light gray through intermediate shadings to black, or from gold through shades of red to liver; always with white on underbody, parts of legs, feet, and part of mask

The Alaskan Malamute is a sociable member of the spitz family named after the Eskimo Mahlemut people who reside by the shores of Kotzebue Sound, a mountainous region in the Arctic Circle. According to stories, this and other similar arctic dogs derive partly from wolves. Whether this is true or not, the Malamute has developed great stamina and speed. It is highly prized as a sled dog, being capable of surviving in arctic temperatures, and of hauling heavy loads over rough terrain.

Despite its rather wolfish appearance, the Alaskan Malamute is a gentle, kind-natured dog, and makes a loyal and devoted companion, but is not very good with other canines. It needs daily brushing and lots of exercise.

Eyes Almond-shaped and brown

Head Broad and powerful

Ears Small in proportion to head

Tail Set moderately high

Body Strong and powerful

Samoyed

The Samoyed or Smiling Sammy takes its name from the Siberian tribe of Samoyedes. This beautiful and devoted spitz variety has great powers of endurance and was one of the breeds used by Fridtjof Nansen and Ernest Shackleton on their expeditions to the North Pole. It has also been used as a guard and to hunt reindeer.

Unlike many sled dogs, the Sammy lives in the homes of its owners in its native land. It is a devoted dog that is good with children and makes an obedient, if slightly independent, housepet. Some breed members have exceled in obedience work. It revels in exercise, and its thick, water-resistant coat needs regular brushing and combing.

Care requirements

4   3   2   1

4   3   2   1

4   3   2   1

4   3   2   1

Pedigree points

Recognized AKC, ANKC, CKC, FCI, KC(GB), KUSA
Height *Dog:* 21–23½ in (52.5–59cm)
Bitch: 19–21 in (47.5–52.5cm)
Weight 50–65 lb (22.5–29.5kg)
Coat Harsh but not wiry, straight, with thick, soft, short undercoat
Color Pure white, white and biscuit, or cream; outer coat silver-tipped

Ears Thick, not too large, and slightly rounded at tips

Head Broad

Eyes Dark and almond-shaped

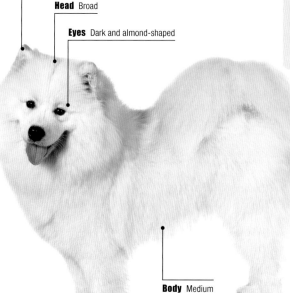

Tail Long, profusely coated, and carried curled over the back

Body Medium length back

Siberian Husky

Care requirements

1 2 3 4

1 2 3 4

1 2 3 4

1 2 3 4

Pedigree points

Recognized AKC, ANKC, CKC, FCI, KC(GB), KUSA
Height *Dog:* 21–23½ in (53–60cm)
Bitch: 20–22 in (51–56cm)
Weight *Dog:* 45–60 lb (20–27kg)
Bitch: 30–50 lb (16–23kg)
Coat Medium in length, giving a well-furred appearance; outer coat straight and lying smooth against body; undercoat soft and dense
Color All colors and markings permissible; markings on head common, including striking ones not found on other breeds

The Siberian Husky was developed in ancient times by the Chukchi people of north-east Asia who wanted a hardy sled dog with strength, speed, and stamina. Wider recognition of its abilities came after the gold rush to Alaska at the turn of the century, when dog-hauled sleds were the only means of transportation available. There was considerable rivalry between the dog teams, and Huskies became famed sled-racing dogs. The breed became renowned during World War II for search and rescue work.

The Siberian Husky is an intelligent and friendly animal with considerable stamina. It is not an aggressive dog and may be kept as a family pet, provided it is given some work and plenty of space and exercise.

Eyes Almond-shaped
Head Medium-sized in proportion to body on an arched neck
Ears Medium-sized
Tail Well-furred and carried gracefully curled over back except when resting
Body Strong with a straight back

Herding Breeds

Newfoundland

There are various theories on the origin of the Newfoundland, but the one that seems most likely is that it is a descendant of the Tibetan Mastiff. In adapting to the rugged conditions in Newfoundland, eastern Canada, it developed webbed feet and an oily coat that allows it to remain in the water for long periods of time. The breed aided fishermen and gained great fame as a life saver. With the strong instinct to rescue anything, or anyone, in the water and retrieve it to safety, it became as valued by crews in Newfoundland waters as the Saint Bernard is by climbers in the Swiss Alps.

A particolored variety of the Newfoundland, known as the Landseer, found fame in the paintings of Sir Edward Landseer. The breed was also much admired by the English poet, Lord Byron.

The large and beautiful Newfoundland is rarely bad tempered unless provoked. Indeed, it is amazingly gentle with other breeds. It does, however, take up a fair amount of space, and needs regular exercise on hard ground and daily brushing using a hard brush.

A gentle giant, the Newfoundland may seem ponderous on land but is in its element in water, swimming strongly and retrieving anything or anyone in its path.

Eyes Small and dark brown

Head Massive and broad

Tail Thick

Ears Small and set well back

Pedigree points

Recognized AKC, ANKC, CKC, FCI, KC(GB), KUSA
Height *Dog:* 28 in (71cm)
Bitch: 26 in (66cm)
Weight *Dog:* 130–150 lb (64–69kg)
Bitch: 110–120 lb (50–54kg)
Coat A double coat that is flat, dense, coarse textured, oily, and water resistant; outer coat moderately long and can be straight or wavy
Color Black, brown, gray, or Landseer (black head with black markings on a white ground)

Body Strong, broad, and muscular

Care requirements

	1	2	3	4
	1	2	3	4
	1	2	3	4
	1	2	3	4

Great Swiss Mountain Dog

The Great Swiss Mountain Dog is the largest of four Swiss mountain dogs, of which the best known is the Bernese. All are thought to descend from Molossus dogs, brought north by ancient Roman armies, and local herding dogs, and they were used for guarding, herding, and draft work. Many have also been used for search and rescue work in the mountains.

The Great Swiss Mountain Dog is a faithful, gentle animal that is generally devoted to children. It is alert and highly intelligent and makes a fine watchdog, willing to protect its human family with its life. It is essentially a country dog that thrives in wide open spaces, and needs plenty of exercise. It requires regular grooming with a bristle brush.

Care requirements

4 3 2 1

4 3 2 1

4 3 2 1

4 3 2 1

Pedigree points

Recognized CKC, FCI
Height *Dog:* 25½–27½ in (65–70cm)
Bitch: 23½–25½ in (59.5–65cm)
Weight *Dog:* 66–70 lb (30–32kg)
Bitch: 55–60 lb (25–27kg)
Coat Stiff and short
Color Black with bright, symmetrical russet and white markings

Eyes Brown and medium-sized

Head Flat and broad

Ears Triangular and medium-sized

Tail Fairly heavy

Body Moderately long, strong, straight back

Appenzell Mountain Dog

Care requirements

1 2 3 4
1 2 3 4
1 2 3 4
1 2 3 4

Pedigree points

Recognized FCI, KUSA
Height *Dog:* 22–23 in (56–58.5cm)
Bitch: 18½–20 in (46–50cm)
Weight 49–55 lb (22–25kg)
Coat Short, dense, and hard
Color Black and tan with white markings on head, chest, and feet; tail tip is always white

The Appenzell Mountain Dog takes its name from a canton in northern Switzerland. The Appenzell is similar in appearance to the Bernese Mountain Dog but is generally smaller, more rectangular in shape, and smooth coated. The Appenzell was used extensively at one time as a herding dog and to haul carts of produce to market. It is still fairly common in its native land, where there is a thriving Appenzell club, but is rarely seen in other countries.

A resilient, intelligent dog that is easily trained, the adaptable Appenzell makes an excellent farm and rescue dog, companion, and guard. It needs plenty of food and exercise, and a daily brushing.

Eyes Brown and rather small

Head Flat, broadest between ears

Ears Fairly small and set high

Tail Medium length, strong, and carried curled over the back

Body Strong, straight back

Hovawart

The Hovawart has been described as a relative newcomer. In fact, the breed has been recognized by the German Kennel Club since 1936, having appeared in Württemberg toward the end of the 19th century. The name Hovawart comes from the German "Hofewart," meaning estate or watch dog, but its role, for many years, seems to have been simply that of a companion dog that will rise to the occasion if required to do so. It has appeared on the European show circuit in recent years and is recognized by the Kennel Club in Britain.

An excellent guard dog that is home loving, fond of children, and easy to train, the Hovawart tends to be a one-person dog. It is slow to mature and will respond aggressively when provoked.

Care requirements

4 3 2 1

4 3 2 1

4 3 2 1

4 3 2 1

Pedigree points

Recognized FCI, KC(GB), KUSA
Height *Dog:* 24–27½ in (63–70cm)
Bitch: 23–25½ in (58–65cm)
Weight *Dog:* 66–88 lb (30–40kg)
Bitch: 55–77 lb (25–35kg)
Coat Medium soft, fairly long, and close to body
Color Black and gold, blond and black

Eyes Brown and medium-sized

Head Strong with broad, convex forehead

Ears Triangular, in proportion with head, and set high

Tail Well-feathered and carried low

Body Longer than height at withers

Care requirements

	1	2	3	4
🐕	1	2	3	4
🥣	1	2	3	4
🪮	1	2	3	4
🏠	1	2	3	4

Pedigree points

Recognized ANKC, CKC, FCI, KC(GB), KUSA

Height *Dog:* 25½–28½ in (65–73cm)
Bitch: 23½–26½ in (60–68cm)

Weight *Dog:* 77–99 lb (35–45kg)
Bitch: 66–88 lb (30–40kg)

Coat Long, plentiful, and rather harsh; never curly

Color All white

Maremma Sheepdog

The Maremma Sheepdog has two names in its native Italy because for centuries the shepherd dogs spent from June until October in the Abruzzi, where there was good summer grazing, and from October until June in the Maremma. Called both Pastore Abruzzese and Pastore Maremmano, some people thought that they were two different breeds. Then, about 25 years ago, a single breed standard was introduced under the name of Pastore Maremmano Abruzzese.

The Maremma is a natural guard that will never forget a kindness or an injury. It should be regularly groomed using a wire brush and, occasionally, a good cleansing powder.

Head Conical, and appears large in proportion to body

Eyes Bold

Ears Small in proportion to head

Body Well-muscled

Tail Set low

Bouvier des Flandres

The Bouvier des Flandres or Belgian Cattle Dog originates, as might be expected, from the Flanders area, between the River Lys valley and the coast. This shaggy dog looks the picture of ferocity in its homeland, where its ears are traditionally cropped. It was bred as a farm dog from a multiplicity of working breeds with the purpose of producing a good all-rounder, and was used in the hunt over rough ground, and as a herder, drover, protector, and guard. The Bouvier has been used extensively as a police dog in Europe.

A possible standard for the breed was discussed in 1912, but it was not until after World War I that a standard was drawn up and finalized by the Club National Belge du Bouvier des Flandres.

The Bouvier des Flandres can be rather fierce, but has a calm and sensible temperament, and is intelligent, hardy, and trustworthy. It is extremely loyal to its family and is easily trained. The breed does, however, require a good deal of exercise and regular brushing. Its somewhat fearsome appearance belies its good nature. It is mainly kept as a pet or show dog.

Descended from ancient rough-coated stock, the Bouvier des Flandres has a steel-wool, all-weather coat. Its ears are usually clipped in its homeland, perhaps to give it a more alert attitude for guarding.

Eyes Alert in expression

Ears Set high

Head Impressive in scale, accentuated by beard and mustache

Tail Usually docked to 2–3 joints

Body Short and strong with broad, deep chest

Pedigree points

Recognized AKC, ANKC, CKC, FCI, KC(GB), KUSA
Height *Dog:* 24½–27½ in (61–69cm)
Bitch: 23½–26½ in (59–66cm)
Weight 88 lb (36kg)
Coat Rough, thick, and harsh with a soft, dense undercoat
Color From fawn to black, including brindle; white star on chest permissible; white predominating or chocolate brown highly undesirable; light, washed-out shades undesirable

Care requirements

Bearded Collie

The Bearded Collie is believed to be one of the oldest herding dogs in Scotland. It may descend from the Komondor of central Europe. Alternately, it may come from three purebred Polish Lowland Sheepdogs—a dog and two bitches—that were exchanged for a ram and a ewe brought by merchants on a trading voyage to Scotland in 1514. Originally, there were two strains of Bearded Collie—the Border dogs, which were gray and white; and the Highland dogs, which were brown and white, and whose coat tended to curl. Interbreeding over hundreds of years has mixed the strains and eliminated the curl.

The Beardie is an alert, self-confident, and active dog, and is good natured and reliable with children. It makes a good pet and a first-class obedience and show dog. It enjoys plenty of exercise, and requires daily brushing, very little combing, and the occasional bath.

Care requirements

4	3	2	1	🐕
4	3	2	1	🥣
4	3	2	1	🖌
4	3	2	1	🏠

Pedigree points

Recognized AKC, ANKC, CKC, FCI, KC(GB), KUSA
Height *Dog:* 21–22 in (53–56cm)
Bitch: 20–21 in (51–53cm)
Weight 40–60 lb (18–27kg)
Coat Flat, harsh, and shaggy; can be slightly wavy but not curly; soft, furry, close undercoat
Color Slate gray, reddish fawn, black, blue, all shades of gray, brown, or sandy, with or without white markings

Eyes Toning with coat color

Head Broad and flat

Ears Medium-sized and drooping

Tail Set low, without a kink or twist

Body Long

Border Collie

Care requirements

1 2 3 4

1 2 3 4

1 2 3 4

1 2 3 4

Pedigree points

Recognized ANKC, CKC, FCI, KC(GB), KUSA
Height *Dog:* 21 in (53cm)
Bitch: slightly less
Weight 30–45 lb (13.5–20kg)
Coat *Two varieties:* moderately long, and smooth; both are thick and straight
Color Variety of colors permissible; white should never predominate

The Border Collie is a descendant of working collies kept in the counties along the border between England and Scotland. It has participated in sheepdog trials since 1873, and has been exported as a working sheepdog all over the world. Bred for stamina and brains, the Border has the natural instinct to herd, and will crouch and circle from puppyhood and learn to work from more experienced dogs. This collie is an unsurpassed contender in agility and obedience work.

Within the past 15 years, the Border Collie has been increasingly chosen as a domestic pet, despite being unsuited to an existence that does not offer sufficient outlet for its energy and intelligence. This loyal working dog requires considerable exercise but only a regular groom with a dandy brush and comb. It must be the ideal choice for anyone with their heart set on winning obedience competitions.

Eyes Oval-shaped and set wide apart

Head Broad skull on slightly arched neck

Ears Medium-sized and set wide apart

Tail Moderately long

Body Athletic

Old English Sheepdog

The Old English Sheepdog has been in existence in Britain for centuries. It is believed to have been developed through the crossing of the Briard with the Russian Owtcharka, which in turn is related to the Hungarian sheepdogs. In the past it was used as a drovers dog and for defending flocks of sheep. In the early 18th century in Britain, drovers dogs were exempt from taxes, and their tails were docked as a means of identification, hence its nickname Bobtail.

The Old English Sheepdog is a kindly dog that gets on well with people, children, and other animals. However, it is fairly large, heavy, and exuberant, and must be given sufficient space and be adequately exercised. Bobtails are popular show dogs but require many hours of grooming.

Care requirements

Pedigree points

Recognized AKC, ANKC, CKC, FCI, KC(GB), KUSA
Height *Dog:* 22 in (56cm)
Bitch: 21 in (53.5cm)
Weight 66 lb (29.5kg) minimum
Coat Profuse but not excessive, and a good, harsh texture
Color Any shade of gray, grizzle, or blue

Eyes Set well apart

Head In proportion to body

Ears Small and carried flat to the side of the head

Tail Docked close to body

Body Short and compact

Care requirements

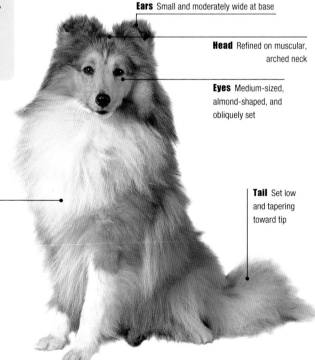

1 2 3 4

1 2 3 4

1 2 3 4

1 2 3 4

Pedigree points

Recognized AKC, ANKC, CKC, FCI, KC(GB), KUSA
Height *Dog:* 14½ in (37cm)
Bitch: 14 in (35.5cm)
Coat Outer coat of long, straight, harsh-textured hair; soft, short-haired, close undercoat
Color Sable, tricolor, blue merle, black and white, or black and tan

Shetland Sheepdog

The Shetland Sheepdog or Sheltie originated in the Shetland Islands off the north coast of Scotland. It resembles a Rough Collie in miniature, with its thick double coat to protect it from the elements in its rigorous native habitat. It is believed to descend from working collies, the Iceland or Yakki Dogs that sometimes reached these islands on whalers, and, possibly, the black and tan King Charles Spaniel.

The Shetland Sheepdog is an excellent choice of family pet for those seeking an intelligent, faithful dog that enjoys exercise, gets on well with children, and makes a fine show and obedience animal. It requires daily grooming using a stiff-bristled brush and a comb. Despite having originated in cold climes, it should not be kenneled outside.

Ears Small and moderately wide at base

Head Refined on muscular, arched neck

Eyes Medium-sized, almond-shaped, and obliquely set

Body Level back

Tail Set low and tapering toward tip

Smooth Collie

The Smooth Collie is identical to the Rough Collie except in coat, that of the Smooth being short and flat, with a harsh-textured top coat and a very dense undercoat. Both Collies' ancestors were brought 400 years ago from Iceland to Scotland, where the breed worked as a sheepdog. Like the Rough, the modern Smooth Collie can trace its ancestry to a tricolor dog called Trefoil that was born in 1873.

The Smooth Collie has the same character and temperament as the Rough, and its care requirements are also the same. Sadly, although the Smooth Collie has all the attributes of the Rough, it is seldom seen. However, the variety does have a dedicated small band of followers and there are many excellent examples with first-class temperaments in the beauty and obedience rings.

Care requirements

4	3	2	1	🐕
4	3	2	1	🍽
4	3	2	1	🧹
4	3	2	1	🏠

Pedigree points

Recognized AKC, ANKC, CKC, FCI, KC(GB), KUSA
Height *Dog:* 22–26 in (56–65cm)
Bitch: 20–24 in (51–60cm)
Weight *Dog:* 45–75 lb (20.5–33.5kg)
Bitch: 40–65 lb (18–29.5kg)
Coat Short, harsh, and smooth, with a dense undercoat
Color Sable and white, tricolor, or blue merle (not permissible in the UK)

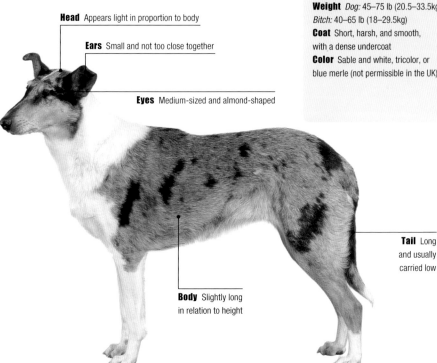

Head Appears light in proportion to body

Ears Small and not too close together

Eyes Medium-sized and almond-shaped

Tail Long and usually carried low

Body Slightly long in relation to height

Rough Collie

Care requirements

1 2 3 4

1 2 3 4

1 2 3 4

1 2 3 4

Pedigree points

Recognized AKC, ANKC, CKC, FCI, KC(GB), KUSA
Height *Dog:* 22–26 in (56–65cm)
Bitch: 20–24 in (51–60cm)
Weight *Dog:* 45–75 lb (20.5–33.5kg)
Bitch: 40–65 lb (18–29.5kg)
Coat Very dense, straight outer coat, harsh to touch, with soft, furry, very close undercoat
Color Sable and white, tricolor, or blue merle (not permissible in the UK)

The Rough Collie, sometimes called the Scots or Scottish Collie, is still best known as the star of the *Lassie* films. This breed's ancestors were introduced into Britain from Iceland more than 400 years ago. The word "colley" is a Scottish term for a sheep with a black face and legs, and the breed worked as a sheepdog in the Highlands of Scotland for centuries. The beauty of the breed was later enhanced, perhaps by the introduction of some Borzoi and Gordon Setter blood. Although it is no longer required to work, it retains its intelligence, hardiness, and keen eyesight.

The Rough Collie makes an excellent guard, being suspicious of strangers. It is supremely loyal and affectionate to its owners, a joy to train, and usually reliable with children. It needs a lot of exercise, but despite its thick coat, it is not difficult to groom.

Eyes Medium-sized and almond-shaped

Head Appears light in proportion to body

Ears Small and not too close together

Tail Long

Body Slightly long in relation to height

Hungarian Puli

The Puli (plural Pulik), one of the best known of the Hungarian sheepdogs, is said to be a descendant of sheepdogs brought to Hungary by the Magyars over 1,000 years ago. It has herded sheep on the edge of the Hungarian plain for many centuries and, more recently, has been used for police work. In 1935, the Puli was imported into the US by the Department of Agriculture with the aim of improving local sheep- and cattle-herding breeds. However, the Puli was not recognized by the American Kennel Club until 1936.

The Puli is a loyal, devoted, obedient, and intelligent dog that is good with other pets and slow to anger. It is, however, reserved with humans outside its own family. The breed requires a good amount of exercise and the cords of its coat, which give it a somewhat unkempt look, have to be separated by hand, brushed, and combed.

Care requirements

4   3   2   1

4   3   2   1

4   3   2   1

4   3   2   1

Pedigree points

Recognized AKC, ANKC, CKC, FCI, KC(GB), KUSA.

Height *Dog:* 16–17½ in (40–44cm)
Bitch: 14½–16 in (37–41cm)

Weight *Dog:* 28½–33 lb (13–15kg)
Bitch: 22–28½ lb (10–13kg)

Coat Dense and weatherproof; outer coat wavy or curly, undercoat soft and woolly; correct proportion of each creates the desired cords

Color Black, rusty black, white, or various shades of gray and apricot; overall appearance of solid color

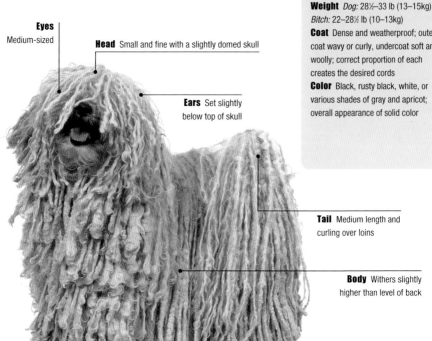

Eyes
Medium-sized

Head Small and fine with a slightly domed skull

Ears Set slightly below top of skull

Tail Medium length and curling over loins

Body Withers slightly higher than level of back

Briard

Pedigree points

Recognized AKC, ANKC, CKC, FCI, KC(GB), KUSA
Height *Dog:* 23–27 in (57.5–67.5cm)
Bitch: 22–25½ in (55–64cm)
Weight 75 lb (33.7kg)
Coat Long, slightly wavy, and dry to the touch, with a fine, dense undercoat
Color Solid black, or with scattered white hairs; fawn, darker shades preferred; fawns may have dark shading on ears, muzzle, back, and tail

The Briard is the best known of the French sheepdogs, the others being the Beauce, Picardy, and Pyrenean. The Briard is reputed to have come to Europe with Asian invaders before the end of the Middle Ages, along with other breeds of sheepdog such as the Hungarian Komondor and Russian Owtcharka, which have similar conformation. The breed became more widely known during World War I, when it carried ammunition for the French Army and was employed by the Red Cross.

The Briard has a gentle nature and makes a good family pet or farm dog, provided sufficient space is available. It is good with children, intelligent, and fearless. It is a breed that takes pride in cleaning itself, but needs regular brushing. Like all sheepdogs, it requires plenty of exercise.

Eyes Dark, set wide apart, and horizontally placed

Head Strong, slightly rounded skull

Ears Set high

Tail Long and well-feathered, with an upward hook at the tip

Body Firm and level back, and a broad chest

Australian Cattle Dog

The Australian Cattle Dog is a superb worker that drives herds by nipping at the cattle's heels. The breed traces back to the now-extinct Black Bobtail, which has been described as large and rather clumsy. In 1840, new blood was introduced, including that of the extinct Smithfield, the native Dingo, the Kelpie, the Dalmatian, and the blue merle Smooth Collie. The Dingo's contributions—keen sense of smell and hearing, stealth, speed, stamina, and tolerance of a dry, hot climate—helped to create this breed uniquely suited to the Australian outback. The addition of Kelpie made it an outstanding heeler as well.

The Australian Cattle Dog is intelligent and good tempered. It is capable of covering immense distances and so requires considerable exercise. It benefits from a vigorous daily brushing.

Care requirements

4	3	2	1	🐕
4	3	2	1	🥣
4	3	2	1	🪮
4	3	2	1	🏠

Pedigree points

Recognized AKC, ANKC, CKC, FCI, KC(GB), KUSA

Height *Dog:* 18–20 in (46–51cm) *Bitch:* 17–19 in (43–48cm)

Weight 35–45 lb (15.5–20kg)

Coat Smooth, hard, straight, water-resistant top coat; short, dense undercoat

Color Blue, blue mottled or blue speckled with or without black, blue, or tan markings on head, evenly distributed for preference; there are other marking requirements; or red speckled with or without darker red markings on head

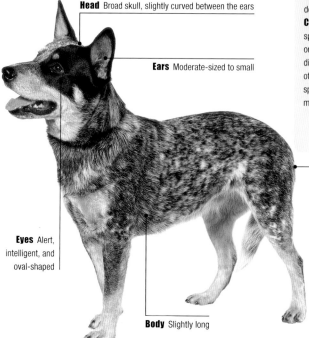

Head Broad skull, slightly curved between the ears

Ears Moderate-sized to small

Tail Set low and follows slope of rump

Eyes Alert, intelligent, and oval-shaped

Body Slightly long

Lancashire Heeler

Care requirements

	1	2	3	4
	1	2	3	4
	1	2	3	4
	1	2	3	4

Pedigree points

Recognized FCI, KC(GB), KUSA
Height *Dog:* 12 in (30cm)
Bitch: 10 in (25cm)
Weight 8–12 lb (3.5–5.5kg)
Coat Short and smooth
Color Black and tan, with rich tan markings on muzzle, in spots on cheeks, and often above eyes, from knees downward, with desirable thumbmark above feet, inside legs, and under tail

The Lancashire Heeler has been known in its native county of England for many years as a sporting dog and dispeller of vermin. As its name suggests, it was developed to herd cattle by nipping at their heels, but also has strong terrier instincts and is an excellent rabbiter and ratter. It is a small dog, and its coat is black with tan markings, although the richness of the tan may fade with age. White is discouraged, except for a very small white spot on the forechest that is permitted but not desirable.

The Lancashire Heeler is a happy, affectionate little dog that gets on well with humans and other pets. It requires an average amount of exercise and daily brushing.

Eyes Medium-sized and almond-shaped

Ears Erect

Head Flat skull

Tail Set high

Body Firm, level topline and well-sprung ribs

Norwegian Buhund

The Norwegian Buhund is a spitz type, and bears a strong resemblance to the Iceland Dog. The Icelandic Sagas record how dogs were brought to Iceland by Norwegian settlers in AD 874. In Norway, the Buhund is used as a guard and farm dog, for herding cattle, sheep, and ponies, and is one of that country's national dogs. Despite its long history, it was little known outside its native land until 1920. Then it reached Britain, where it has never become really popular but does have a band of ardent devotees. It has been developing a following in other countries, but is not yet recognized in the US.

The Norwegian Buhund is a natural herder. It is also a gentle, friendly dog, and a natural guard and reliable playmate for children. It needs a fair amount of exercise, and daily brushing and combing.

Care requirements

4	3	2	1
4	3	2	1
4	3	2	1
4	3	2	1

Pedigree points

Recognized ANKC, CKC, FCI, KC(GB), KUSA
Height *Dog:* 17–18 in (42.5–45cm)
Bitch: smaller
Weight 26–40 lb (12–18kg)
Coat Close, harsh, and smooth, with a soft, woolly undercoat
Color Wheaten, black, red, or wolf-sable; small symmetrical white markings permissible; black mask

Head Light, and broad between the ears

Eyes Dark brown and oval-shaped

Ears Set high

Tail Short, thick, set high, and carried tightly curled over back

Body Strong and short

Swedish Vallhund

Pedigree points

Recognized ANKC, FCI, KC(GB), KUSA
Height *Dog:* 13–13¾ in (33–35cm)
Bitch: 12–13 in (31–33cm)
Weight 25–35 lb (11.5–16kg)
Coat Medium length, harsh, and close, with a soft, woolly undercoat
Color Steel gray, grayish brown, grayish yellow, reddish yellow, or reddish brown; darker guard hairs on back, neck, and sides of body; lighter shade of same color desirable on muzzle, throat, chest, belly, buttocks, feet, and hocks; white markings acceptable in place of lighter shades but never in excess of one-third of coat

The Swedish Vallhund is known in its native land as Västgötaspets, which means "spitz of the West Goths." It closely resembles the Welsh Corgis, although the Vallhund is somewhat higher in the leg and shorter in the back. Undoubtedly there is a connection between the breeds, but whether Corgis taken by the Vikings to Sweden developed into the Vallhund or Swedish dogs brought to Britain developed into Corgis is not known. Like the Corgi, the Vallhund is a splendid cattle dog.

The Swedish Vallhund is a friendly, loyal, affectionate little dog, described in its standard as active and eager to please. It makes a good family pet and needs plenty of exercise.

Eyes Medium-sized

Head Rather long

Ears Medium-sized and pointed

Tail If present, should not exceed 4 in (10cm) in adults; puppies born with tails may be docked

Body Level back and well-muscled

Welsh Corgi Pembroke

The Welsh Corgi Pembroke, a favorite of British royalty, has worked in South Wales at least since the time of the Domesday Book, instigated by William the Conqueror in the 11th century. Its job was to control the movement of cattle by nipping their ankles, which is an inherent characteristic that many protectors of the British royal family have discovered to their cost. The breed may have been introduced to Wales by Flemish weavers who settled in the area and crossed their own dogs with local stock.

Corgis are extremely active and devoted little dogs, and are usually good with children. They make fine guards, and excellent show and obedience dogs. They have a tendency to put on weight if under-exercised, and their water-resistant coats need daily brushing.

Care requirements

4   3   2   1

4   3   2   1

4   3   2   1

4   3   2   1

Pedigree points

Recognized AKC, ANKC, CKC, FCI, KC(GB), KUSA
Height 10–12 in (25.5–30.5cm)
Weight *Dog:* 27 lb (12kg)
Bitch: 25 lb (11.5kg)
Coat Medium length and straight, with a dense undercoat; never soft, wavy, or wiry
Color Red, sable, fawn, or black and tan, with or without white markings on legs, brisket, and neck; some white on head and foreface permissible

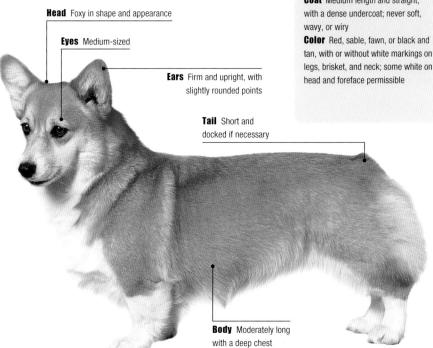

Head Foxy in shape and appearance

Eyes Medium-sized

Ears Firm and upright, with slightly rounded points

Tail Short and docked if necessary

Body Moderately long with a deep chest

Welsh Corgi Cardigan

Pedigree points

Recognized AKC, ANKC, CKC, FCI, KC(GB), KUSA

Height 10½–12½ in (26–31cm)

Weight *Dog:* 30–38 lb (13.5–17kg)
Bitch: 25–34 lb (11.5–15.5kg)

Coat Short or medium length, with a hard texture, and weatherproof; short, thick undercoat

Color Any, with or without white markings, but white should not predominate

The rarer Welsh Corgi Cardigan is believed to have been brought to the high hills of Cardiganshire in Wales by the Celts when they emigrated from central Europe around 1200 BC. It is readily distinguishable from the tailless or docked Pembroke by its fox-like brush. The Cardigan is functionally built, being strong, agile, and tough enough to drive and herd wild cattle, dairy cows, and mountain ponies. It also helped to find and hunt game, and served as a child's guardian and companion. The Welsh Corgis were first exhibited in Britain in 1925, and the Pembroke and Cardigan received separate classification in 1934.

The Cardigan is said to have a slightly more equable temperament than the Pembroke and is possibly less bold. It requires firmness and consistency from its owner to avoid behavior problems, and does well in obedience competition and at agility.

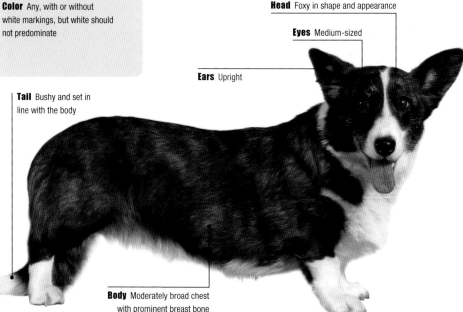

Head Foxy in shape and appearance

Eyes Medium-sized

Ears Upright

Tail Bushy and set in line with the body

Body Moderately broad chest with prominent breast bone

Anatolian Shepherd Dog

The Anatolian Shepherd Dog, previously known as the Anatolian Karabash, has existed for centuries, from the Anatolian plateau of Turkey right across Afghanistan. Such large, powerful, and heavy headed dogs have lived in the area since Babylonian times and were once used as war dogs and to hunt big game such as lions and even horses. However, their more usual job was to guard sheep, and shepherds would crop their ears and fit them with spiked collars to help them defend flocks from predators.

This powerful, loyal, and loving dog is good with children, makes a fine watchdog, and is eminently trainable. However, it cannot be kept in a confined space, is not suited to town life, and does not take kindly to strangers. It requires considerable exercise, and should be brushed regularly.

Care requirements

4	3	2	1
4	3	2	1
4	3	2	1
4	3	2	1

Pedigree points

Recognized ANKC, FCI, KC(GB), KUSA
Height *Dog:* 29–32 in (74–81cm)
Bitch: 28–31 in (71–79cm)
Weight *Dog:* 110–141 lb (50–64kg)
Bitch: 90½–130 lb (41–59kg)
Coat Short and dense, with a thick undercoat
Color All acceptable, but most desirable is solid cream to fawn with black mask and ears

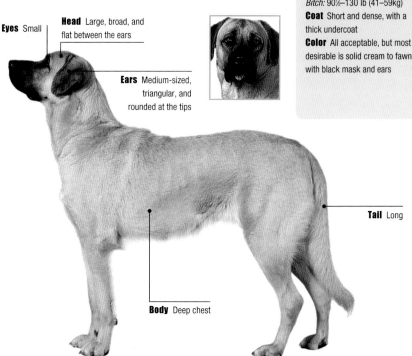

Eyes Small

Head Large, broad, and flat between the ears

Ears Medium-sized, triangular, and rounded at the tips

Tail Long

Body Deep chest

Care requirements

	1	2	3	4
1	2	3	4
1	2	3	4
1	2	3	4

Pedigree points

Recognized AKC, ANKC, CKC, FCI, KC(GB), KUSA

Height *Dog:* 24–26 in (60–65cm)
Bitch: 22–24 in (55–60cm)

Weight 75–95 lb (33.5–42.5kg)

Coat Medium length, straight, hard and close, with a dense, thick undercoat

Color Solid black or gray; black saddle with tan or gold to light gray markings; gray with lighter or brown markings (referred to as sables); blues, livers, albinos, and whites highly undesirable (a light-coated German Shepherd is included in the breed standards of some countries)

German Shepherd Dog

It has been suggested that the German Shepherd Dog, or Alsatian, may be a descendant of the Bronze Age wolf. Certainly, around the 7th century, there existed in Germany a shepherd dog of similar type but with a lighter coat. By the 16th century, the coat is said to have darkened appreciably.

The German Shepherd is extremely intelligent and makes a first-class companion, show dog, and guard. It is eminently trainable and so works as a police dog and as a guide dog for the blind. Its superior guarding ability can get it into trouble, because it may misread a sign and spring to its owner's defence. It needs daily grooming, plenty of exercise, and above all a job to do, even if this only entails competing in obedience or agility tests. It is unfair and unwise for this intelligent animal to be subjected to a life of boredom.

Head Strong on a relatively long neck

Ears Medium-sized

Eyes Medium-sized

Tail Long and bushy

Body Straight back, long shoulder blades, and strong, broad, well-muscled hindquarters

Belgian Shepherd Dogs

This breed includes four varieties: the Groenendael (long-coated black), the Tervueren (long-coated other than black), the Malinois (smooth-coated), and the Laekenois (wire-coated). All were developed from the many sheepdogs of varying colors and sizes that existed in Belgium toward the end of the 19th century. They are recognized as separate breeds everywhere except in the UK.

The medium-sized, well-proportioned, intelligent, and attentive Belgian Shepherd Dog works well in obedience trials and makes an excellent guard. It is very protective, and can be kept in the home provided time is set aside for early training. It needs plenty of exercise and regular grooming.

Pedigree points

Recognized AKC, ANKC, CKC, FCI, KC(GB), KUSA

Height *Dog:* 24–26 in (61–66cm) *Bitch:* 22–24 in (56–61cm)

Weight 62 lb (28kg)

Coat *Groenendael & Tervueren:* long, straight, and abundant, with an extremely dense undercoat *Malinois:* very short on head, exterior of ears, and lower parts of legs; short on rest of body *Laekenois:* harsh, wiry, and dry

Color *Groenendael:* black; black with limited white (small to moderate patch or strip on chest, between pads of feet, and on tips of hind toes); frosting (white or gray) on muzzle *Tervueren:* all shades of red, fawn, gray, with black overlap *Malinois:* all shades of red, fawn, gray, with black overlap *Laekenois:* reddish fawn with black shading, principally on muzzle and tail

Head Finely chiseled

Ears Distinctly triangular, stiff, and erect

Eyes Medium-sized

Tail Medium length, firmly set, and strong at the base

Body Powerful but elegant, with a broad chest

Groenendael

The most popular of the Belgian Shepherd Dogs, the Groenendael was named by Monsieur Rose of the Café du Groenendael, who developed the breed.

Malinois

First to establish type among the motley of Belgian Shepherd Dogs was the Malinois, which is named after its region of origin.

Laekenois

The Laekenois, the rarest of the four breeds, comes from the district of Boom, near Antwerp.

Tervueren

The Tervueren is also named after its region of origin. The Tervueren fawn factor occasionally occurs in a litter of light-colored Groenendaels.

Care requirements

	1	2	3	4
1	2	3	4
1	2	3	4
1	2	3	4

Gundogs

Labrador Retriever

The Labrador Retriever does not come from Labrador but from Newfoundland, Canada, where it was used to help fishermen land their nets. The dogs are thought to have originated in Devon, England, and to have been taken to North America by fishermen. In the 1830s, Newfoundland fishermen reimported the dogs into England, and it is these dogs that formed the basis of the breed as we know it.

The Labrador Retriever is a first-class gundog and fine swimmer, and ideally combines the role of pet and sporting companion. It is a worthy contender in obedience competitions, draws large entries in the show ring, and works as a guide dog for the blind. Exuberant in youth, but easy to train, the Labrador is good with children and rarely seems to get into any kind of trouble. It needs plenty of exercise and regular brushing, and can be kept either in or outdoors.

Care requirements

4   3   2   1

4   3   2   1

4   3   2   1

4   3   2   1

Pedigree points

Recognized AKC, ANKC, CKC, FCI, KC(GB), KUSA

Height *Dog:* 22½–24½ in (56–61cm)
Bitch: 21½–23½ in (54–59cm)

Weight *Dog:* 60–75 lb (27–33.5kg)
Bitch: 55–70 lb (25–33.5kg)

Coat Short and dense, without wave or feathering; weather-resistant undercoat

Color Wholly black, yellow, or liver/chocolate; yellows range from light cream to red fox; a small white spot on the chest is permissible

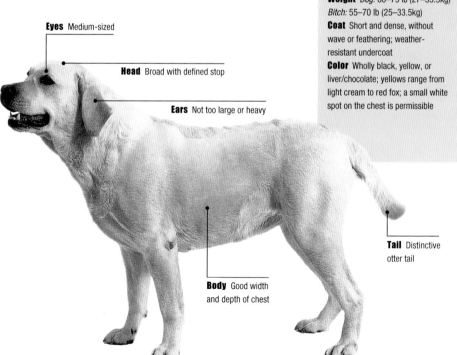

Eyes Medium-sized

Head Broad with defined stop

Ears Not too large or heavy

Tail Distinctive otter tail

Body Good width and depth of chest

Golden Retriever

Pedigree points

Recognized AKC, ANKC, CKC, FCI, KC (GB), KUSA
Height *Dog:* 22–24 in (56–61cm)
Bitch: 20–22 in (51–56cm)
Weight *Dog:* 65–75 lb (29.5–33.5kg)
Bitch: 55–65 lb (25–29.5kg)
Coat Flat or wavy with good feathering and a dense, water-resistant undercoat
Color Any shade of gold or cream, but neither red nor mahogany; a few white hairs on the chest are permissible

Some dog breeds owe their existence to the dedicated work of one individual, and such is the case with the Golden Retriever. Lord Tweedmouth, from the Scottish Highlands, was responsible for developing the breed from retriever/spaniel stock in the 1850s. He wanted a dog that could work in heavy cover, swim strongly, and retrieve from cold water. These abilities, together with the dog's happy nature, helped to ensure its enormous worldwide popularity.

The Golden Retriever perfectly combines the roles of sportsman's companion and family pet, being an excellent gundog, of sound temperament, and gentle with children. It is also a popular show dog that works well in obedience competitions. Requiring regular brushing and ample exercise, the Golden Retriever is best suited to a country environment. It will, however, adapt to suburban conditions provided that good walks and a garden are available.

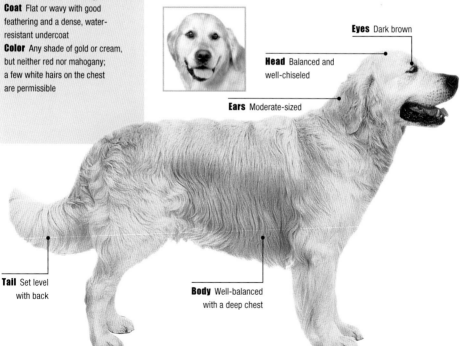

Eyes Dark brown

Head Balanced and well-chiseled

Ears Moderate-sized

Tail Set level with back

Body Well-balanced with a deep chest

Curly-coated Retriever

Everything about the Curly-coated Retriever points to the Irish Water Spaniel or the Standard Poodle contributing to its ancestry. The Labrador Retriever also played some part in producing this fine breed.

The Curly-coated Retriever has an excellent nose and a good memory. It is a better guard than other retrievers, and while a little anti-social with its canine colleagues in the shooting field, it generally combines its working life admirably with that of a reliable family dog. It requires vigorous exercise, and fares best in a country environment. Its curly coat does not need to be brushed or combed, just dampened down and massaged with circular movements. Advice should be sought on the necessary trimming for exhibitions.

Care requirements

Pedigree points

Recognized AKC, ANKC, CKC, FCI, KC(GB), KUSA
Height *Dog:* 27 in (67cm)
Bitch: 25 in (62cm)
Weight 70–80 lb (31.5–36.5kg)
Coat A mass of crisp, small curls all over, except on face
Color Black or liver

Eyes Black or dark brown

Head Long and well-proportioned

Ears Small and set low

Tail Carried straight

Body Muscular shoulders and deep chest

Flat-coated Retriever

Care requirements

	1	2	3	4
	1	2	3	4
	1	2	3	4
	1	2	3	4

Pedigree points

Recognized AKC, ANKC, CKC, FCI, KC(GB), KUSA
Height *Dog:* 23–24 in (58–61cm)
Bitch: 22–23 in (56–59cm)
Weight *Dog:* 60–80 lb (25–35kg)
Bitch: 55–70 lb (25–34kg)
Coat Dense, fine to medium texture, medium length, and lying flat
Color Solid black or solid liver

Once known as the Wavy-coated Retriever, the breed is thought to have evolved from the Labrador Retriever and spaniels. It is likely that collie blood was introduced to produce the flat coat. The Flat-coat is superlative at picking up game, and it is an excellent wildfowler and water dog. It is loyal and affectionate, and although it can be kept as a pet, most Flat-coats are maintained for the job for which the breed was originally bred and they are happiest when doing this.

An intelligent dog with a kindly temperament, it is a hardy breed and many owners choose to keep their Flat-coats in outside kennels, although this is a matter of preference. Like most gundogs, Flat-coats need plenty of exercise and a daily brushing.

Eyes Medium-sized

Head Long and clean

Ears Small, well-set, and lying close to side of head

Tail Straight and well-set

Body Strong with deep chest

Chesapeake Bay Retriever

The ancestry of the Chesapeake Bay Retriever is less obscure than that of many breeds. Indeed, its origins can be pinpointed to 1807, when an English brig was shipwrecked off the coast of Maryland. An American ship, the *Canton*, rescued the English crew and two Newfoundland puppies. One puppy was a male called Sinbad, which has been described as dingy red in color, while the other was a black bitch, which became known as Canton after the rescue ship. The pups were presented to the families that had given shelter to the English sailors and were trained as duck retrievers. In time, they mated with various working breeds in the Chesapeake Bay area. It is likely that the cross bloods added were those of the Otterhound and the Curly-coated and Flat-coated Retrievers. The matings produced a variety with the swimming ability of the Newfoundland and the duck-retrieving abilities of local dogs.

Until fairly recently, the Chesapeake Bay Retriever was kept strictly as a sporting dog. However, it is now finding its way into the family home and becoming a contender in the show ring.

The Chesapeake is good natured and does well in field trials. It has an oily coat that needs regular brushing and gives off a slight, but not unpleasant, odor. It has yellow-orange eyes. Like all gundogs, it needs plenty of exercise and does best in an environment where it has space to roam freely.

Yellow-amber eyes are a characteristic of the Chesapeake Bay Retriever, as well as the waviness on the neck, back, and loins.

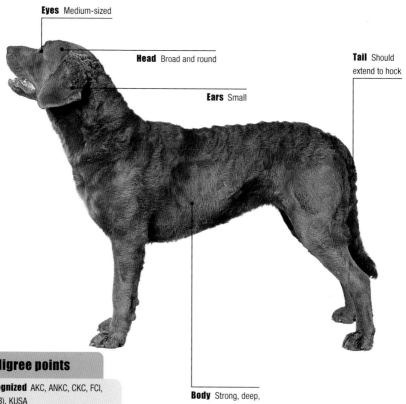

Eyes Medium-sized

Head Broad and round

Ears Small

Tail Should extend to hock

Body Strong, deep, broad chest

Pedigree points

Recognized AKC, ANKC, CKC, FCI, KC(GB), KUSA
Height *Dog:* 23–26 in (58.5–66cm)
Bitch: 21–24 in (53.5–61cm)
Weight *Dog:* 65–80 lb (29.5–36.5kg)
Bitch: 55–70 lb (25–32kg)
Coat A distinctive feature; thick, not over 1½ in (2cm) long, with harsh, oily outer coat and dense, fine, woolly undercoat
Color Dead grass (straw to bracken), sedge (red-gold), or any shade of brown; white spots (the smaller the better) on chest, toes, and belly permissible

Care requirements

	1	2	3	4
	1	2	3	4
	1	2	3	4
	1	2	3	4

Nova Scotia Duck Tolling Retriever

The Nova Scotia Duck Tolling Retriever originated in the Maritime Provinces of Canada. It is believed to be of Chesapeake Bay and Golden Retriever stock. With the head of the Golden, it is well boned down to its strong webbed feet. This dog's job in life is to thrash about at the water's edge in order to attract the attention of wildfowl, a performance known as tolling. Eventually the wildfowl become curious or angry enough to swim within range of the hunter on the bank. The dog will retrieve the fowl shot down.

The Nova Scotia Duck Tolling Retriever is quiet and easy to train. Like many gundogs, it makes a good pet provided that it receives plenty of exercise. It needs regular grooming with a bristle brush and comb.

Care requirements

4　3　2　1

4　3　2　1

4　3　2　1

4　3　2　1

Pedigree points

Recognized ANKC, CKC, FCI, KC(GB)
Height 17–21 in (41–52cm)
Weight 37–51 lb (16.5–23kg)
Coat Moderately long and close, with a thick, wavy undercoat
Color Red fox, with white markings on chest, feet, and tip of tail, and sometimes on face

Ears Triangular and set high

Head Broad with well-defined stop

Eyes Almond-shaped

Tail Broad at base, luxuriant, and well-feathered

Feet Webbed

Clumber Spaniel

Care requirements

	1	2	3	4

Pedigree points

Recognized AKC, ANKC, CKC, FCI, KC(GB), KUSA
Height *Dog:* 19–20 in (48–50cm)
Bitch: 17–19 in (42.5–48cm)
Weight *Dog:* 70–85 lb (31.5–38kg)
Bitch: 55–70 lb (25–31.5kg)
Coat Abundant, close, and silky
Color Plain white body with lemon markings preferred; orange permissible; slight head markings and freckled muzzle

The Clumber is the heaviest of the spaniels, with the Basset and the now extinct Alpine Spaniel in its ancestry. It is a reliable, slow, but sure dog mainly confined to country areas where it excels in flushing game over rough ground and as a retriever. In the years just prior to the French Revolution, the Clumber was promoted by the Duc de Noailles and became renowned as a beater and retriever. At the beginning of hostilities, the French Duke brought his dogs to England and entrusted them to the Duke of Newcastle at Clumber Park, near Nottingham, from which the breed gets its name. The French Duke met his death in the Revolution but the breed lived on.

The Clumber is of good temperament and may be kept as a pet, but its ideal role is as a working gundog in the countryside. It needs a fair amount of brushing, and care must be taken that mud does not become lodged between its toes.

Eyes Clean dark amber, slightly sunk

Head Massive, square, and medium length

Ears Large and vine-leaf shaped

Tail Set low

Body Long, heavy, and close to ground, with a deep chest

American Cocker Spaniel

The name of the American Cocker Spaniel is derived from the predilection of the English Cockers for "cocking," or hunting woodcock. The breed was of Spanish origin, but the American Cocker can be traced back to an English-bred bitch, Obo Obo, brought over from Britain in the 1880s.

The English Cocker Spaniel Club of America, formed in 1935, helped establish the breed. It is distinguished by its small stature—suited to the lighter New World game birds—shorter head, and extremely dense coat. This smallest of American gundogs, and the most popular breed in the country, was recognized by the AKC in 1946 as the American Cocker Spaniel. For many years the American Cocker was shown exclusively in the ring. Recently, however, field trials have been reintroduced.

The American Cocker has a much thicker coat than the English Cocker and elegant trousers. It is a useful, all-purpose gundog, able both to flush out and retrieve. It is a popular show dog, makes a fine housepet, and is usually good with children. The American Cocker needs plenty of exercise, daily brushing and combing, and if it is the desire to exhibit, fairly intricate trimming using scissors and electric clippers.

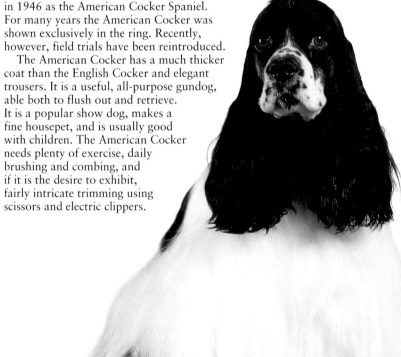

Careful attention is needed to the American Cocker Spaniel's long, silky coat, which is much thicker than that of the English Cocker.

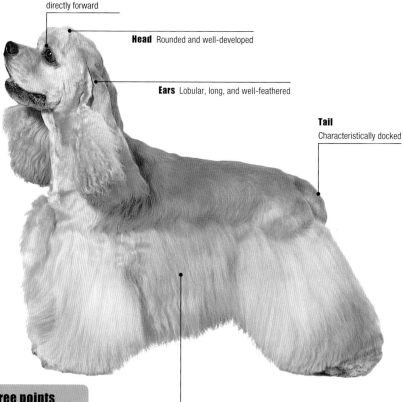

Eyes Full and looking directly forward

Head Rounded and well-developed

Ears Lobular, long, and well-feathered

Tail Characteristically docked

Pedigree points

Recognized AKC, ANKC, CKC, FCI, KC(GB), KUSA

Height *Dog:* 14½–15½ in (36.5–39cm)
Bitch: 13½–14½ in (34–36.5cm)

Weight 24–28 lb (11–12.5kg)

Coat Short and fine on head, medium length on body, with enough undercoat to give protection

Color Black or jet black, with shadings of brown or liver in sheen of coat undesirable; black and tan, or brown and tan, with definite tan markings on jet black or brown body; particolors and tricolors

Body Back slopes slightly downward from shoulders to tail

Care requirements

	1	2	3	4
	1	2	3	4
	1	2	3	4
	1	2	3	4

English Cocker Spaniel

The Cocker Spaniel is also called the Merry Cocker because of its wagging tail. It originated in Spain (the word "spaniel" comes from *Espagnol*, meaning Spanish). Spaniels have been known since the 14th century and were used in falconry. In the 19th century, the breed came into its own in the task of flushing out woodcock and small game, and became known as the cocking or Cocker Spaniel.

The English Cocker Spaniel is a gentle and popular pet, as well as being a first-class gundog, which is able both to flush out and retrieve. It needs careful brushing and combing every day, and immense care must be taken to dislodge any mud that may have become caked in its paws or its ears. Some owners gently peg back their spaniel's ears when it is eating.

Care requirements

4	3	2	1	🐕
4	3	2	1	🍽
4	3	2	1	🧹
4	3	2	1	🏠

Pedigree points

Recognized AKC, ANKC, CKC, FCI, KC(GB), KUSA
Height *Dog:* 15½–17 in (39–42.5cm)
Bitch: 15–16 in (38–41cm)
Weight 28–32 lb (12.5–14.5kg)
Coat Flat and silky
Color Various; self (pure) colors, no white allowed on chest

Eyes Full but not prominent

Head Square muzzle

Ears Lobular, long, and well-feathered

Tail Set slightly lower than line of back

Body Strong and compact

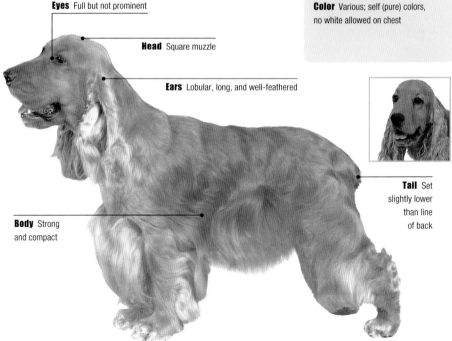

Care requirements

1 2 3 4

1 2 3 4

1 2 3 4

1 2 3 4

Pedigree points

Recognized AKC, ANKC, CKC, FCI, KC(GB), KUSA
Height *Dog:* 18–19 in (45–48cm)
Bitch: 17–18 in (42.5–45cm)
Weight 35–45 lb (16–20kg)
Coat Straight, flat, and silky; some feathering on chest, underside of body, and legs
Color Rich red and white only

Welsh Springer Spaniel

The Welsh Springer Spaniel, or its forerunner, is mentioned in the earliest records of the Laws of Wales, dating back to about 1300. It is also possible that these red and white spaniels are a cross between the English Springer and the Clumber. Certainly, the breed has the Brittany in its ancestry, being similar both in its ability as a gundog and in conformation.

This loyal and hard-working gundog is somewhere between the English Cocker Spaniel and the English Springer Spaniel in size. It is a good swimmer, has an excellent nose, and combines the role of family dog and sportsman's companion provided the need for exercise is met. It needs brushing daily, and regular checks to make sure that mud does not become lodged in its paws or ears.

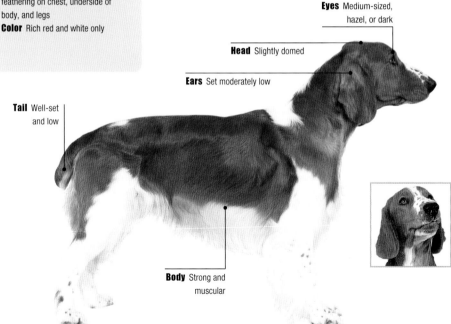

Eyes Medium-sized, hazel, or dark

Head Slightly domed

Ears Set moderately low

Tail Well-set and low

Body Strong and muscular

English Springer Spaniel

The English Springer is one of the oldest of the British spaniels, with the exception of the Clumber. The land spaniel written about in 1570 by the historian Dr Caius was obviously a forerunner of the Springer. It was originally used for flushing or springing game from cover before shotguns were in use. For a time it was known as the Norfolk Spaniel, named after either a Norfolk family that kept a strain of "springing" spaniels prior to 1900 or the breed's place of origin in the county of Norfolk in England.

Sir Thomas Boughey, who helped establish the modern breed, had Springers with a pedigree traceable to a bitch that whelped in 1812. Sir Thomas's family retained an interest in the breed until the 1930s and many of today's field trials champions are descendants of his strain. The English Springer Spaniel Club was formed in the UK in 1921, but the breed had found fame as a "bird dog" in the United States long before.

The English Springer Spaniel is an intelligent, loyal, and popular gundog that also makes a reliable housepet and is good with children. The breed needs plenty of exercise, a daily brushing, and regular checks to ensure that mud does not become lodged in its paws or its ears. The Springer may not be a good choice for the house proud because it tends to have a good shake when it comes indoors out of the rain.

Spaniels bred to flush game were often known as "springers," because in effect they sprang from cover. Outstanding in the field, the English Springer is also a good family pet.

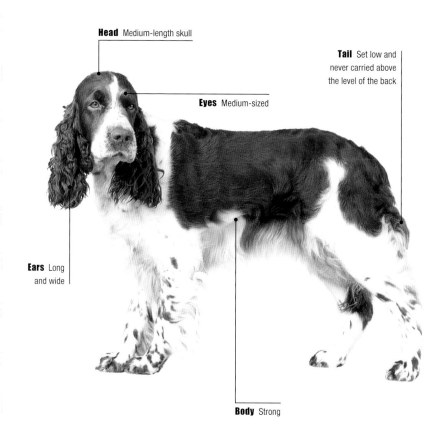

Head Medium-length skull

Tail Set low and never carried above the level of the back

Eyes Medium-sized

Ears Long and wide

Body Strong

Pedigree points

Recognized AKC, ANKC, CKC, FCI, KC(GB), KUSA
Height *Dog:* 20 in (51cm)
Bitch: 19 in (48.5cm)
Weight 49–55 lb (22–25kg)
Coat Close, straight, and weather-resistant; never coarse
Color Liver and white, black and white, or either of these with tan markings

Care requirements

	1	2	3	4
	1	2	3	4
	1	2	3	4
	1	2	3	4

Irish Water Spaniel

Documentary evidence for water dogs traces back to AD 17, and water spaniels have been known in Ireland for more than a millennium. The Irish Water Spaniel is thought to have developed through crosses with Poodles and Curly-coated Retrievers. Prior to 1859, there were two separate strains of the breed, one in the north and one in the south. The southern strain, which resembled the Standard Poodle, probably formed the basis of the modern breed.

The Irish Water Spaniel is a brave, loving, and intelligent animal. Maintaining its coat of curls is not such a chore as might be expected. However, it does need to be groomed at least once a week using a steel comb. Some stripping of unwanted hair is necessary, as is trimming around the feet.

Care requirements

4	3	2	1
4	3	2	1
4	3	2	1
4	3	2	1

Pedigree points

Recognized AKC, ANKC, CKC, FCI, KC(GB), KUSA

Height *Dog:* 21–24 in (53–60cm)
Bitch: 20–23 in (51–58cm)

Weight *Dog:* 55–65 lb (25–29.5kg)
Bitch: 45–58 lb (20–26kg)

Coat Dense, tight ringlets on neck, body, and top part of tail; longer, curling hair on legs and topknot; face, rear of tail, and back of legs below hocks smooth

Color Rich, dark liver

Eyes Small and almond-shaped

Head Good-sized and high-domed on a long, arching neck

Ears
Long and
oval-shaped

Tail
Short

Body Deep chest

Sussex Spaniel

Pedigree points

Recognized AKC, ANKC, CKC, FCI, KC(GB), KUSA
Height 13–16 in (32.5–40cm)
Weight 35–50 lb (15.7–23kg)
Coat Abundant and flat, without a tendency to curl; ample weather-resistant undercoat
Color Rich, golden liver shading to golden at tips of hairs, gold predominating; dark liver or puce is undesirable

Once popular with farmers, Sussex Spaniels have been known in the county of Sussex in southern England for around two centuries. The breed was originated by a Mr Fuller of Rosehill, Sussex, in 1795. It was first exhibited at Crystal Palace, London, in 1862. Later a bigger strain, known as the Harvieston, was developed. This owed something to the Clumber Spaniel and the Bloodhound, and to this day some Sussex Spaniels have a hound look about them. The Sussex is used mainly for partridge and pheasant.

The Sussex is a working spaniel with an excellent nose, and makes an ideal country dog. It tends to attach itself to one person, and is loyal and easy to train. It requires a daily brush and comb, and as with all spaniels, care must be taken that mud does not become caked in its ears and feet.

Eyes Fairly large, hazel-colored, with a soft expression

Head Wide and slightly rounded between the ears

Ears Fairly large and thick

Body Deep, well-developed chest

Tail Set low and never carried above level of back

Field Spaniel

The Field Spaniel has the same origin as the Cocker Spaniel, being, in effect, a larger version of it, and early litters sometimes contained both. Then in 1892, the varieties went their separate ways. While the Cocker was improved greatly, the Field Spaniel was bred to produce an exaggeratedly long body and short legs, and its popularity and numbers declined sharply.

In 1948 the Field Spaniel Society was reformed in Britain and considerable work was undertaken by dedicated enthusiasts. This resulted in a better proportioned standard type evolving that is breeding true and producing some very nice specimens. Despite this, the Field Spaniel is still rarely seen in its country of origin outside the show ring. It is recognized in the US, but very few specimens are registered there.

The Field Spaniel has an equable temperament and makes a good household pet and gundog. Like other spaniels, it thrives on plenty of exercise, and needs to be brushed and combed every day, taking care that its coat does not become matted.

The Field Spaniel shares its origins with the Cocker Spaniel, although the two types became separate breeds in 1892. At one time bred for extreme characteristics, the Field Spaniel has been rehabilitated over the past half century.

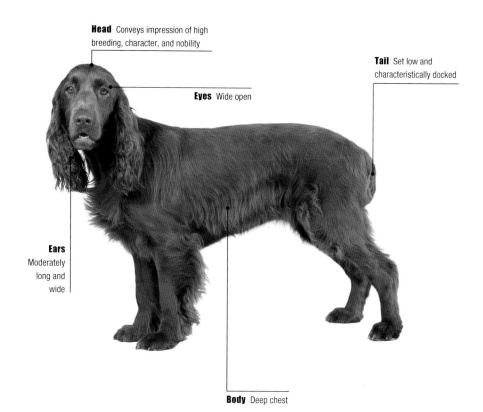

Head Conveys impression of high breeding, character, and nobility

Eyes Wide open

Tail Set low and characteristically docked

Ears Moderately long and wide

Body Deep chest

Pedigree points

Recognized AKC, ANKC, CKC, FCI, KC(GB), KUSA
Height *Dog:* 18 in (45–47cm)
Bitch: 17 in (42.5cm)
Weight 35–55 lb (15.5–25kg)
Coat Long, flat, silky, and glossy, without curls
Color Black, liver, or roan with tan markings; clear black, white, or liver and white unacceptable

Care requirements

1   2   3   4

1   2   3   4

1   2   3   4

1   2   3   4

English Setter

Prior to the introduction of firearms for hunting, various methods were employed to catch game birds. Dogs were trained to seek birds and then to crouch motionless near them until the hunter arrived and threw a net. This type of dog became known as a setter, because it would sit or "set" when it found the birds. The English, which has been known since the 14th century, is the oldest and most distinctive of the four breeds of setter, the others being the Irish, the Gordon, and the Irish Red and White.

Loyal and affectionate, the English Setter admirably combines the role of family pet and sportsman's dog. It is good with children, can live as one of the family or outdoors, and needs only daily brushing with a stiff brush and the use of a steel comb. Straggly hairs must be removed before exhibition. Like most gundogs, it requires plenty of exercise.

Care requirements

4	3	2	1
4	3	2	1
4	3	2	1
4	3	2	1

Pedigree points

Recognized AKC, ANKC, CKC, FCI, KC(GB), KUSA
Height *Dog:* 25–27 in (62–68cm)
Bitch: 24–25 in (60–62cm)
Weight 40–70 lb (18–31.5kg)
Coat Short, straight, and dense
Color Black and white (blue belton), orange and white (orange belton), lemon and white (lemon belton), liver and white (liver belton), or tricolor (blue belton and tan or liver belton and tan); those without heavy patches of color but flecked (belton) all over are preferred

Eyes Neither deep nor prominent

Head Lean and noble

Ears Set moderately low

Body Short, level, and well-muscled back and high withers

Tail Set almost in line with back, softly feathered, and scimitar-shaped

Gordon Setter

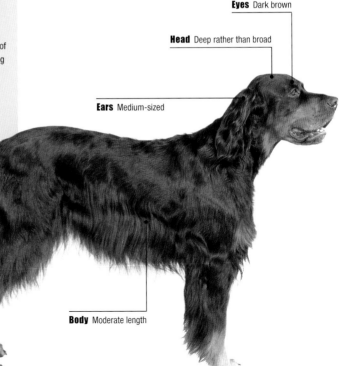
Pedigree points

Recognized AKC, ANKC, CKC, FCI, KC(GB), KUSA

Height *Dog:* 24–27 in (60–70cm)
Bitch: 23–26 in (57–65cm)

Weight *Dog:* 55–80 lb (25–36.5kg)
Bitch: 45–70 lb (20–31.5kg)

Coat Short and fine on head, fronts of legs, and tips of ears; moderately long over rest of body; flat and curl-free

Color Deep, shining coal black, without rustiness, and with lustrous tan (chestnut red) markings; black penciling on toes and black streak under jaw permissible

The Gordon, formerly the Gordon Castle Setter, owes its existence to Alexander, Fourth Duke of Richmond and Gordon, who bred Scotland's only gundog in the late 1770s. He aimed to produce a larger, heavier setter by introducing Bloodhound and, it is widely thought, collie blood. Gordons are not so fast or stylish as other setters.

The Gordon is a tireless worker, able to withstand the heat of grouse shooting in the height of summer better than other setters, and able to work without water for longer. It will combine the role of gundog admirably with that of a family pet and it is a better watchdog than other setters. The Gordon needs plenty of space and lots of exercise, and is not best suited to town life.

Eyes Dark brown

Head Deep rather than broad

Ears Medium-sized

Tail Straight or slightly curved, not too long

Body Moderate length

Irish Setter

The Irish Red Setter (or Big Red) was developed through the crossing of Irish Water Spaniels, Spanish Pointers, and both the English and Gordon Setters. This resulted in a beautiful, exuberant, pointer-like dog. Although it originated in Ireland, the breed came into its own in Victorian England, where its speed and energy, developed for the conditions found in Ireland, made it ideally suited to work as a gundog in large, open expanses of countryside.

While undoubtedly having hunting ability, this breed is widely sought as a popular and loving family pet. It is good with children and other pets, and has a particular affinity with horses. The Irish Setter has boundless energy and, therefore, needs plenty of exercise, as well as a daily brushing. It will adapt to a suburban home, but is far better suited to country life where it has plenty of freedom.

Care requirements

4	3	2	1	🐕
4	3	2	1	🥣
4	3	2	1	🪮
4	3	2	1	🏠

Pedigree points

Recognized AKC, ANKC, CKC, FCI, KC(GB), KUSA
Height 25–27 in (63.5–68.5cm)
Weight 60–70 lb (27–31.5kg)
Coat Short and fine on head, fronts of legs, and tips of ears; moderately long, free, and as straight as possible on rest of body; good feathering
Color Rich chestnut with no trace of black; white markings on chest, throat, chin, or toes, or small star on forehead or narrow streak or blaze on nose or face permissible

Head Long and lean

Eyes Dark hazel to dark brown

Ears Moderate-sized

Tail Moderate in length in relation to size of body

Body Chest as deep as possible, and rather narrow in front

Irish Red and White Setter

The Irish Red and White Setter evolved from spaniels, probably red and white spaniels, that were brought to Ireland from France and crossed with pointers, and by the 18th century, Red and White Setters were being bred to type. Then setter fanciers began to prefer the Irish Setter, and by the end of the 19th century, the Red and White all but disappeared. Since the 1940s the breed has undergone a revival in Ireland.

The Irish Red and White Setter is a happy, good-natured, and affectionate dog that admirably combines the role of sportsman's dog and family pet. It needs space and plenty of exercise, and requires daily brushing.

Care requirements

- 🐕 1   2   3   4
- 🥣 1   2   3   4
- 🪮 1   2   3   4
- 🏠 1   2   3   4

Pedigree points

Recognized ANKC, FCI, KC(GB), KUSA
Height 23½–27 in (59–67cm)
Weight 40–70 lb (18–31. 5kg)
Coat Flat, straight, and finely textured with good feathering
Color Clearly particolored with pearl white base and solid red patches; mottling and flecking, but not roaning, permitted around face and feet, and up foreleg to elbow and up hind leg as far as hock

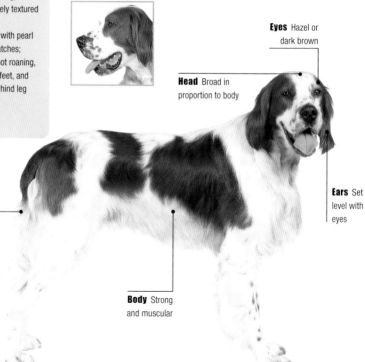

Eyes Hazel or dark brown

Head Broad in proportion to body

Ears Set level with eyes

Tail Strong at root and tapering to fine point

Body Strong and muscular

Brittany

The Brittany, formerly known as the Brittany Spaniel, is the only spaniel in the world that points to game. It is a fine woodcock dog and will also retrieve wildfowl. Believed to have originated in Spain or the Argoat forests of Brittany, it has also been suggested that the Brittany may be the progeny of an English Red and White Setter dog and a Breton bitch. In the 1800s, a popular pastime for English gentry was woodcock-hunting in France. Most brought their own dogs, and inevitably some of these pointers and setters bred with native spaniels.

The Brittany has high energy, intelligence, and great affection for its family. It does not respond well to rough handling, but gentle handling reaps rewards. It requires daily brushing and plenty of exercise.

Care requirements

4	3	2	1	🐕
4	3	2	1	🥣
4	3	2	1	🪮
4	3	2	1	🏠

Pedigree points

Recognized AKC, ANKC, CKC, FCI, KC(GB), KUSA
Height 17½–20½ in (44–51cm)
Weight 30–40 lb (13.5–18kg)
Coat Body coat flat and dense, never curly; a little feathering on legs
Color Orange and white or liver and white in clear or roan patterns, or tricolor (also black and white in the UK)

Eyes Expressive

Head Rounded and medium length

Ears Dropped

Tail Naturally short or usually docked to 4 in (10cm), with a small twist of hair on the end, carried level with the back

Body Deep chest reaching to the level of the elbows

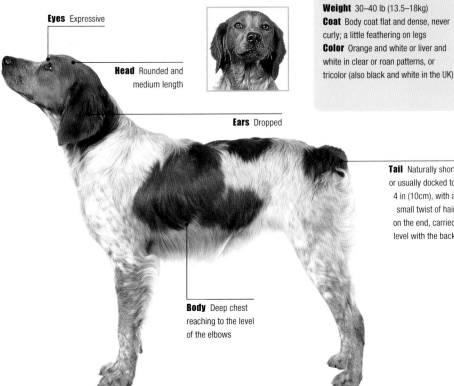

Pointer

Pedigree points

Recognized AKC, ANKC, CKC, FCI, KC(GB), KUSA

Height *Dog:* 25–28 in (62.5–70cm)
Bitch: 23–26 in (57.5–65cm)

Weight *Dog:* 55–75 lb (25–33.5kg)
Bitch: 45–65 lb (20–29.5kg)

Coat Short, dense, and smooth

Color Lemon and white, orange and white, liver and white, or black and white; self (pure) colors and tricolors also correct

Like the setters, the Pointer is famed for its classic stance, pointing with nose and tail in the direction of game. It is thought by many to have originated in Spain. There is, however, a school of thought that it may be of English origin, developed through crossings of Foxhound, Bloodhound, and Greyhound. Early Pointers were hard-headed dogs, unwilling to submit to control. In the early 1800s, they were crossed with setters to improve their disposition, making them more amenable to working with people.

The Pointer is a popular show dog, and admirably combines the roles of sportsman's companion and family pet. It is an affectionate, obedient dog that is easy to train, good with children, and needs only regular brushing to keep its coat in good condition. It does, however, need plenty of exercise and so is not ideally suited to town life.

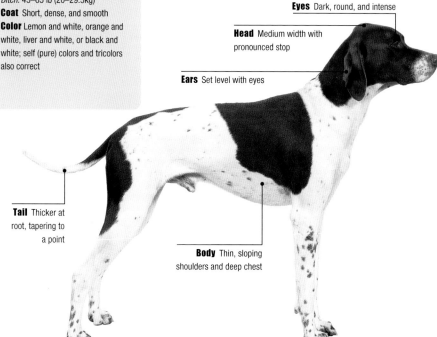

Eyes Dark, round, and intense

Head Medium width with pronounced stop

Ears Set level with eyes

Tail Thicker at root, tapering to a point

Body Thin, sloping shoulders and deep chest

German Short-haired Pointer

The German Short-haired Pointer is of Spanish origin, probably derived through crossing the Spanish Pointer with a scenthound to produce a versatile gundog that would both point and trail. English Foxhound blood is also believed to have been added.

The German Short-haired Pointer is a powerful, strong, and versatile hunting dog. It is equally at home on land or in the water, and excellent at working wildfowl and most game. It also makes a good household pet, provided that it receives enough exercise. It is easy to train, usually good with children, and does not require a lot of grooming.

Care requirements

4	3	2	1	🐕
4	3	2	1	🍽
4	3	2	1	🧹
4	3	2	1	🏠

Pedigree points

Recognized AKC, ANKC, CKC, FCI, KC(GB), KUSA
Height *Dog:* 23–25 in (58–64cm)
Bitch: 21–23 in (53–59cm)
Weight *Dog:* 55–70 lb (25–31.5kg)
Bitch: 45–60 lb (20–27kg)
Coat Short, flat, and coarse
Color Solid liver, liver and white spotted, or liver and white spotted and ticked; liver and white ticked; the same variations with black instead of liver; not tricolored

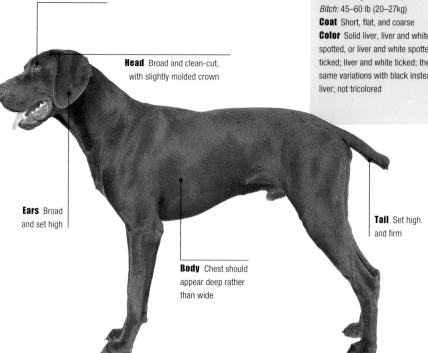

Eyes Medium-sized

Head Broad and clean-cut, with slightly molded crown

Ears Broad and set high

Body Chest should appear deep rather than wide

Tail Set high and firm

German Wire-haired Pointer

The German Wire-haired Pointer is very similar to the German Short-haired Pointer, except in coat, and the latter obviously had a hand in the Wire-haired's make-up, as did the Wire-haired Pointing Griffon and the Stichelhaar, as well as the Airedale Terrier. The German Wire-haired Pointer was claimed to be superior to the Short-haired in forest and water, and at hunting bigger game. Although popular in its homeland, the German Wire-haired took longer than the Short-haired to become established overseas.

The Wire-haired, although it can adapt to the role of household pet, has had certain aggressive qualities bred into it, and is best kept purely as a hunting dog.

Head Broad with slightly rounded crown

Eyes Medium-sized and oval-shaped

Ears Medium-sized in relation to head

Body Chest should appear deep rather than wide

Tail Starts high and thick, growing gradually thinner toward tip

Weimaraner

The Weimaraner, or Silver Ghost, bears a striking resemblance to a painting by Van Dyck (circa 1631). However, it is said to have been purpose-bred as a gundog in the 1800s by the Grand Duke Karl August of the German city-state of Weimar, after which the breed is named. Breeds that are likely to have played a part in its make-up include the Saint Hubert or other French hounds, Short-haired Pointers, Spanish Pointers, Bloodhounds, and German Schweisshunds. The result is a fine gundog that was originally used against big game, and more recently as a police dog.

The Weimaraner is good natured and distinctive looking, with a metallic silver-gray coat and amber or blue-gray eyes. It excels in obedience and agility, and makes a fine pet provided that it has an outlet for its keen intelligence. It is best housed indoors rather than in a kennel and requires little grooming.

Care requirements

4	3	2	1	🐕
4	3	2	1	🥣
4	3	2	1	🖌
4	3	2	1	🏠

Pedigree points

Recognized AKC, ANKC, CKC, FCI, KC(GB), KUSA
Height *Dog:* 24–27 in (61–69cm)
Bitch: 22–25 in (56–64cm)
Weight 70–85 lb (31.5–38kg)
Coat Short, smooth, and sleek
Color Preferably silver gray; shades of mouse or roe gray permissible

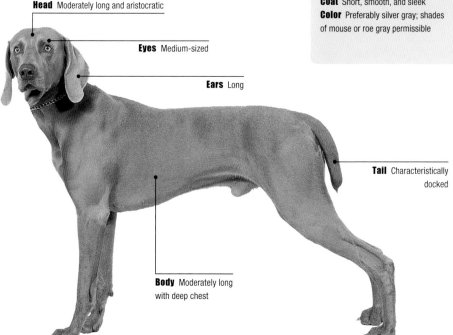

Head Moderately long and aristocratic

Eyes Medium-sized

Ears Long

Tail Characteristically docked

Body Moderately long with deep chest

Hungarian Vizsla

Pedigree points

Recognized AKC, ANKC, CKC, FCI, KC(GB), KUSA
Height *Dog:* 22½–25 in (57–64cm)
Bitch: 21–23½ in (53–60cm)
Weight 48½–66 lb (20–30kg)
Coat Short, dense, and straight
Color Russet gold; small white marks on chest and feet acceptable

The Hungarian Vizsla is the national hunting dog of Hungary. This smooth-haired setter was bred on the central Hungarian plain, the habitat of a wide variety of game. The Vizsla was developed as an extremely versatile dog, able to hunt, track, point, and retrieve hares, ducks, geese, and other prey. It is likely that the German Weimaraner, to which it bears a strong resemblance, and Transylvanian pointing dogs played a part in its early development. However, Magyar noblemen took immense care not to introduce new blood that might prove detrimental to the ability of this breed.

The Vizsla is a versatile, easily trained gundog that also makes a first-class pet and is good with children. It needs plenty of exercise and its coat should be brushed regularly.

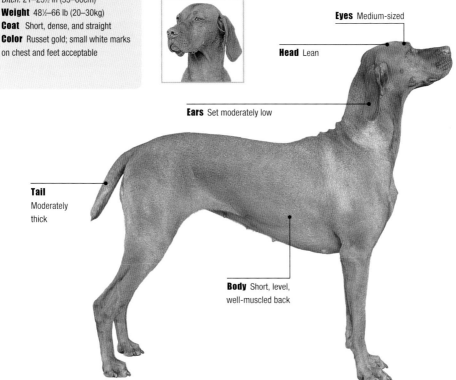

Eyes Medium-sized

Head Lean

Ears Set moderately low

Tail Moderately thick

Body Short, level, well-muscled back

Gundogs
Kooikerhondje

This breed is also known as the Kooiker Dog or Duck-decoy Dog. Its Dutch name means "dog belonging to the Kooiker," the person in charge of the duck decoy. It is a fairly old breed, native to the Netherlands, whose job was to draw ducks out of their cover by walking in and out of low reed fences by the banks of a dyke that was covered with netting. When the ducks investigated, the dyke was closed.

The Kooikerhondje is an intelligent, affectionate dog that is lively but not over-excitable. A good companion dog, it is a handy size for a household pet. It needs plenty of exercise and daily brushing.

Care requirements

4	3	2	1	🐕
4	3	2	1	🥣
4	3	2	1	🖌
4	3	2	1	🏠

Pedigree points

Recognized FCI
Height 15 in (38cm)
Weight 20–24 lb (9–11kg)
Coat Moderately long and slightly wavy; feathering on chest, legs, and tail
Color Clear white with red patches

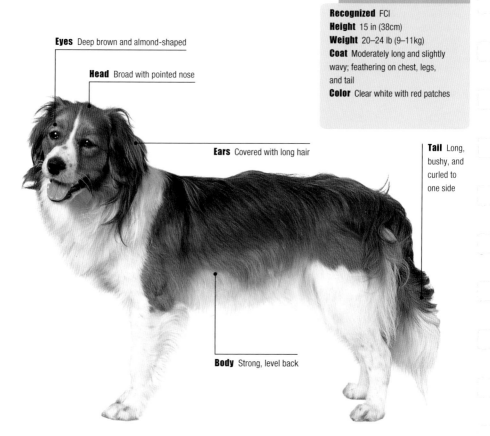

Eyes Deep brown and almond-shaped

Head Broad with pointed nose

Ears Covered with long hair

Tail Long, bushy, and curled to one side

Body Strong, level back

Italian Spinone

Care requirements

1 2 3 4

1 2 3 4

1 2 3 4

1 2 3 4

Pedigree points

Recognized AKC, ANKC, CKC, FCI, KC(GB), KUSA

Height *Dog:* 23½–27½ in (59–69cm)
Bitch: 23–25½ in (57.5–64cm)

Weight *Dog:* 70–82 lb (32–37kg)
Bitch: 62–71 lb (28–32kg)

Coat Rough, thick, and fairly wiry

Color White, white with orange markings, solid white peppered orange, white with brown markings, or white speckled with brown (brown roan), with or without brown markings

The Italian Spinone is an ancient gundog breed. However, it has only recently become a contender in the international show ring and in field trials. Opinions vary, even in Italy, about the dog's origin, as to whether it is of setter descent—climatic conditions alone accounting for its thick coat—or a relative of the coarse-haired Italian Segugio or, indeed, a Griffon cross. Other authorities believe that this powerful, versatile hunter originated in the French region of Bresse, later finding its way to Piedmont in Italy, and that its evolution is attributable not only to the French Griffon, but also to German Pointers, the Porcelaine, the now extinct Barbet, and the Korthals Griffon. Or the Spinone may be the result of a mating between a Coarse-haired Setter and a white mastiff.

Affectionate, agreeable, and of loyal temperament, the Italian Spinone has a soft mouth and will both point and retrieve. It needs plenty of vigorous exercise, is a fine swimmer, and is best suited to country life.

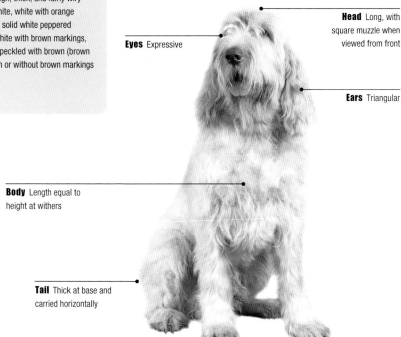

Head Long, with square muzzle when viewed from front

Eyes Expressive

Ears Triangular

Body Length equal to height at withers

Tail Thick at base and carried horizontally

Münsterländer

Münsterländers combine the best qualities of the setter and the spaniel, having the setter's build and the spaniel's head. While officially recorded as one of the newest pointing and retrieving gundog breeds, the Large Münsterländer has been well established in its native Germany as an all-purpose gundog since the beginning of the 18th century. Then it was regarded as a German Long-haired Pointer, but in the early days of the German Kennel Club it was decided that only brown and white German Long-haired Pointers would be eligible for registration and pups of other colors were given away. The "odd-colored" puppies fell into the hands of farmers whose aim was to perpetuate the best working qualities, irrespective of color. Thus, the farmers were able to build up and save an interesting and attractive variety of gundog, known today as the Large Münsterländer.

The Small Münsterländer is a more recent breed, derived by crossing the Brittany with the German Long-haired Pointer in the early 20th century.

Münsterländers are loyal, affectionate, and trustworthy dogs that admirably fulfill the roles of sportsman's companion and family pet. They are energetic and so need plenty of exercise, and a daily brushing.

The Large Münsterländer is an all-purpose pointing/ retrieving dog, but also makes an excellent family pet.

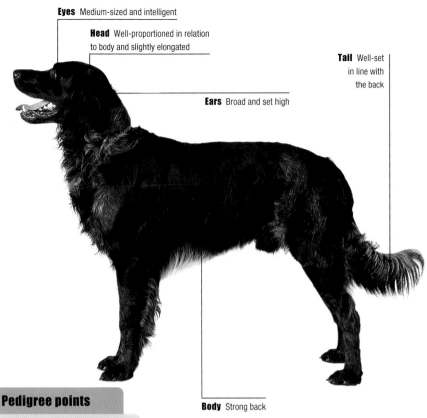

Eyes Medium-sized and intelligent

Head Well-proportioned in relation to body and slightly elongated

Tail Well-set in line with the back

Ears Broad and set high

Body Strong back

Pedigree points

Recognized *Large:* ANKC, FCI, KC(GB), KUSA *Small:* FCI, KC(GB)
Height *Large dog:* 24 in (61cm) *Large bitch:* 23 in (58–59cm) *Small:* 19–22 in (47.5–55cm)
Weight *Large dog:* 55–65 lb (25–29kg) *Large bitch:* 55 lb (25kg) *Small:* 33 lb (15kg)
Coat Moderately long and dense, with feathering
Color *Large:* head solid black, white blaze, strip, or star allowed; body white or blue roan with black patches, flecks, ticks, or a combination of these *Small:* liver and white with ticking

Care requirements

	1	2	3	4
	1	2	3	4
	1	2	3	4
	1	2	3	4

Hounds

Pharaoh Hound

The Pharaoh Hound is a medium-sized sight breed that will also hunt by scent. It has been described as the oldest domesticated dog in recorded history because it so closely resembles the likenesses of dogs carved on the tomb walls of the pharaohs and on ancient Egyptian artefacts dating back to at least 2000 BC. In 1935, archeologists working in the great cemetery west of the Pyramid of Cheops, at Giza, found an inscription recording that such a dog, named Abuwtiyuw, had been buried with all the ritual ceremony of a great man of Egypt by order of the kings of Upper and Lower Egypt.

It is thought that these hounds were taken to Malta and Gozo by the Phoenicians. First imported into the UK in the 1920s, the breed was re-established in Britain in 1968 when eight examples were imported from Gozo and Malta, and it was soon recognized. It was introduced into North America in the late 1960s and was subsequently recognized.

The affectionate and intelligent Pharaoh Hound has a happy, confident personality, likes children, and makes a good family pet. Its coat needs little attention but the breed does require plenty of exercise and is not suited to cramped conditions.

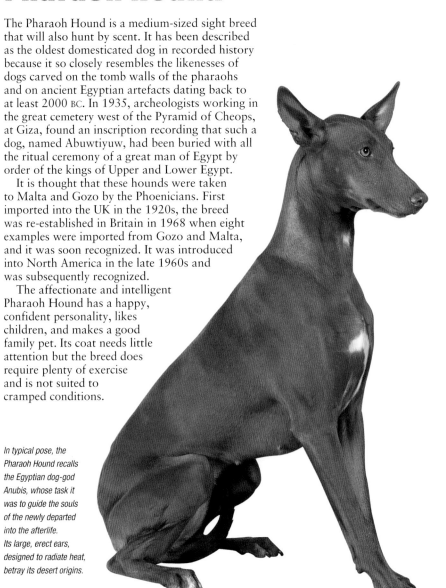

In typical pose, the Pharaoh Hound recalls the Egyptian dog-god Anubis, whose task it was to guide the souls of the newly departed into the afterlife.
Its large, erect ears, designed to radiate heat, betray its desert origins.

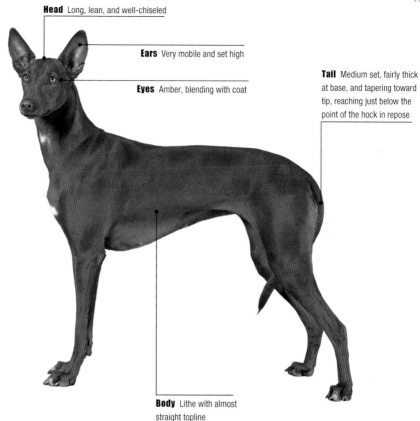

Head Long, lean, and well-chiseled

Ears Very mobile and set high

Eyes Amber, blending with coat

Tail Medium set, fairly thick at base, and tapering toward tip, reaching just below the point of the hock in repose

Body Lithe with almost straight topline

Pedigree points

Recognized AKC, ANKC, CKC, FCI, KC(GB)
Height *Dog:* 22–25 in (55–62.5cm)
Bitch: 21–24 in (52.5–60.5cm)
Coat Short and glossy
Color Tan or rich tan with white markings; white tip on tail strongly desirable; white star on chest, white on toes, and slim white blaze on center line of face permissible; flecking or white other than above undesirable

Care requirements

	1	2	3	4
	1	2	3	4
	1	2	3	4
	1	2	3	4

Ibizan Hound

4	3	2	1	
4	3	2	1	
4	3	2	1	
4	3	2	1	

Like the Pharaoh Hound, the Ibizan Hound is descended from hunting dogs kept by the ancient Egyptians. In the 9th century BC, Egypt was invaded by the Romans, and the neighboring Carthaginians and Phoenicians were driven out to the island of Ibiza. The hounds they took with them remained on Ibiza for the next 3,000 years, still retaining the colors depicted on Egyptian drawings of their ancestors. The breed was also used for hunting in southern Spain and France. The Ibizan Hound comes in three varieties: smooth-, coarse-, and long-haired.

This noble-looking animal has a kindly nature, is good with children, rarely fights, and makes a fine gundog or housepet. It is extremely sensitive and has acute hearing, so must never be shouted at, but responds well to kind treatment. Like all hounds, it needs a lot of exercise. Its coat is easy to maintain, needing only a daily brushing.

Pedigree points

Recognized AKC, ANKC, CKC, FCI, KC(GB), KUSA
Height *Dog:* 23½–27½ in (59–69cm)
Bitch: 22½–26 in (56–65cm)
Weight *Dog:* 50 lb (22.5kg)
Bitch: 45 lb (20kg)
Coat Smooth or rough; always hard, close, and dense
Color Solid white, chestnut, or lion, or any combination of these

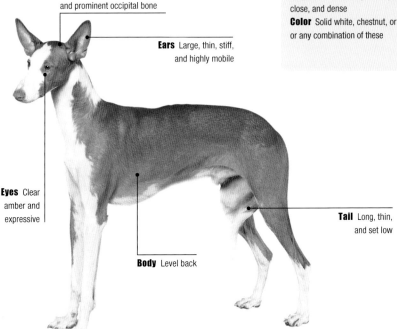

Head Long, fine, with flat skull and prominent occipital bone

Ears Large, thin, stiff, and highly mobile

Eyes Clear amber and expressive

Tail Long, thin, and set low

Body Level back

Care requirements

- 🐾 1 2 3 4
- 🥣 1 2 3 4
- 🖌 1 2 3 4
- 🏠 1 2 3 4

Pedigree points

Recognized AKC, ANKC, CKC, FCI, KC(GB), KUSA

Height *Dog:* 17 in (43cm)
Bitch: 16 in (40cm)

Weight *Dog:* 24 lb (11kg)
Bitch: 22 lb (10kg)

Coat Short, sleek, close, and very fine

Color Black, red, or black and tan; all should have white on chest, feet, and tail tip; white blaze, collar, and legs optional; black and tan with tan melon pips and black, tan, and white mask

Basenji

The Basenji (meaning "bush thing") comes from central Africa and is also called the Zande Dog, Belgian Congo Dog, Congo Bush Dog, Bongo Terrier, Congo Terrier, and Nyam Nyam Terrier. Its likeness is depicted on the tombs of the pharaohs. Used as a hunting dog in its native land, the Basenji is famed for the fact that it does not bark, instead giving a kind of yodel. European explorers came upon the breed in the mid-19th century in the Congo and southern Sudan.

The Basenji is playful, extremely loving, dislikes wet weather, and needs a reasonable amount of exercise. It washes itself like a cat and has no doggie smell, so a daily rub-down with a hound glove will suffice. The bitch comes into season only once a year, and pups may be destructive if unchecked.

Head Flat, well-chiseled, and proudly carried

Eyes Dark and almond-shaped

Ears Small, pointed, erect, and slightly rounded

Tail Set high, curling tightly over spine and lying close to thigh, with a single or double curve

Body Well-balanced with short, level back

Hamiltonstövare

The Hamiltonstövare or Hamilton Hound is named after Count Adolf Patrick Hamilton, founder of the Swedish Kennel Club, who standardized the breed about a century ago. This medium-sized hound, used to flush game in the forests of Sweden, resulted from cross-breedings between the English Foxhound, the Holstein Hound, the Hanoverian Haidbracke, and Hanover and Kurland Beagles (now extinct). Hamiltonstövare is currently the most popular hunting hound in its native land.

This smart, affectionate, and intelligent dog makes a good companion that may be kept in the home, provided that it receives plenty of exercise. It needs daily grooming using a hound glove.

Care requirements

4	3	2	1	
4	3	2	1	
4	3	2	1	
4	3	2	1	

Pedigree points

Recognized ANKC, FCI, KC(GB), KUSA
Height *Dog:* 19½–23½ in (50–60cm)
Bitch: 18–22½ in (46–57cm)
Weight 50–60 lb (22.5–27kg)
Coat Strongly weather-resistant upper coat lying close to body; short, close, soft undercoat
Color Upper side of neck, back, sides of trunk, and upper side of tail: black; head, legs, side of neck, trunk, and tail: brown; blaze on upper muzzle, underside of neck, breast, tip of tail, and feet: white; mixing of black and brown, or predominance of any one of the three colors is undesirable

Eyes Expressive and clear amber

Head Fine, long, and flat

Ears Large, thin, and stiff

Tail Long, thin, and set low

Body Level back

Pedigree points

Recognized AKC, ANKC, CKC, FCI, KC(GB), KUSA
Height *Dog:* 25–27 in (63–67.5cm)
Bitch: 23–25 in (58–63cm)
Weight *Dog:* 90–110 lb (40.5–48.5kg)
Bitch: 80–100 lb (36.3–45kg)
Coat Smooth, short, and weatherproof
Color Black and tan, liver (red) and tan, or red

Bloodhound

The Bloodhound or Chien de Saint Hubert is one of the oldest hound breeds. It is generally believed that its earliest ancestors were dogs bred in Assyria around 2000–1000 BC. Taken to the Mediterranean region by Phoenician traders, it then spread through Europe. A concentration of hounds developed in Brittany in the 7th and 8th centuries, from which emerged the Saint Hubert. Able to follow a days-old scent, the Bloodhound will not kill its quarry once found.

Good with children and exceedingly affectionate, the Bloodhound makes an ideal companion for those who have the room to accommodate it, the energy to exercise it, and neighbors who do not object to its baying. It can be kept in an average-sized home provided that it has adequate exercise, but is best suited to a rural environment. It should be groomed daily with a hound glove.

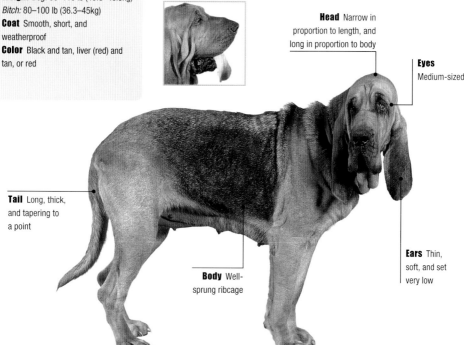

Head Narrow in proportion to length, and long in proportion to body

Eyes Medium-sized

Tail Long, thick, and tapering to a point

Body Well-sprung ribcage

Ears Thin, soft, and set very low

Otterhound

The big, strongly built British Otterhound is believed to trace back to the Griffon Vendéen and the now extinct rough-coated Griffon de Bresse. According to the Otterhound Club, these hounds were imported into Britain in significant numbers before 1870. Shortly afterward, the Comte le Couteuix de Canteleu sent his entire pack of Griffons to a Mr Richard Carnaby Forster, who gave them to his stepdaughter, Lady Mary Hamilton. In 1906, the Hamilton Otterhounds were sold individually to masters of Otterhounds.

The Otterhound is a shaggy breed with a majestic head framed by long, pendulous ears.

The Otterhound has keen scenting abilities almost on a par with the Bloodhound. The dogs, which are fine swimmers, would swim upriver, following the otter's "wash" (trail of bubbles). When otter hunting was outlawed in the UK in the late 1970s, the Master of the Kendal and District Otterhounds in the Lake District set up the Otterhound Club to ensure the breed's survival.

The Otterhound makes an amiable though stubborn pet that can be somewhat destructive within the household, if undisciplined. Like other thick-coated breeds, it can be kenneled outdoors if the owner wishes, though many Otterhounds do live indoors. It needs a considerable amount of exercise and its rough coat should be groomed once a week, and bathed as necessary.

Head Clean and very imposing

Ears Long, pendulous (a unique feature of the breed), and set level with corner of eyes

Tail Set high and carried up when alert or moving

Eyes
Intelligent

Body Well-sprung ribcage

Pedigree points

Recognized AKC, ANKC, CKC, FCI, KC(GB), KUSA
Height *Dog:* 24–27 in (60–67.5cm)
Bitch: 23–26 in (57.5–65cm)
Weight *Dog:* 75–115 lb (33.5–51.5kg)
Bitch: 65–100 lb (29.5–45kg)
Coat Long (1½–3 in/4.5cm), dense, rough, and harsh, but not wiry
Color All hound colors permissible

Care requirements

	1	2	3	4
	1	2	3	4
	1	2	3	4
	1	2	3	4

Italian Segugio

The Italian Segugio comes in two coat types, short-haired and coarse-haired. The origins of this ancient Italian hunting dog trace back to the coursing dogs of ancient Egypt and it still has something of the Greyhound in its appearance. As well as having keen eyesight, it is blessed with an exceptional sense of smell, and was used against a wide variety of game. Today it is used mainly to hunt hare. The Segugio will remain bravely within firing distance once it has found its quarry.

It can cope with most types of terrain, and is a natural hunter, but it should be trained in its working role during its early months. It is generally good natured, if a little strong willed, and can be kept as a companion dog. It needs plenty of exercise, but its coat needs little attention apart from regular brushing.

Care requirements

4   3   2   1

4   3   2   1

4   3   2   1

4   3   2   1

Pedigree points

Recognized FCI, KC(GB)
Height *Dog:* 21–23 in (53–58.5cm)
Bitch: 19–22 in (48–56cm)
Weight 39–62 lb (17.5–28kg)
Coat Dense, glossy, and smooth; or coarse on head, ears, body, legs, and tail
Color Various shades of red, fawn, or black and tan

Eyes Large and luminous

Head Elongated and narrow

Tail Set high in line with croup

Ears Flat, and should hang and be flat for almost their entire length

Body Length of body from shoulder to buttock should equal height at withers

Care requirements

1 2 3 4

1 2 3 4

1 2 3 4

1 2 3 4

Pedigree points

Recognized AKC, ANKC, CKC, FCI, KC(GB), KUSA
Height *Dog:* 25–26½ in (63–67cm)
Bitch: 24–26 in (61–66cm)
Weight 65–75 lb (29.5–33.5kg)
Coat Short, dense, sleek, and glossy
Color Light wheaten to red wheaten

Rhodesian Ridgeback

The local Khoikhoi people of southern Africa went on hunting expeditions accompanied by a dog with a ridge of hair growing in the reverse direction along its back. During the 16th and 17th centuries, European immigrants brought Pointers, Mastiffs, Greyhounds, and Bulldogs, which crossed with the Ridgeback. The Rhodesian Ridgeback was named after the country of Rhodesia (now Zimbabwe), where it was highly valued by the settlers. It was also known as the Lion Dog because it was used in packs to hunt lions.

This attractive animal is obedient, good with children, and will guard its owner with its life. It has a gentle temperament but can move with great speed when it spies a rabbit or other prey. It needs plenty of exercise and daily grooming with a hound glove.

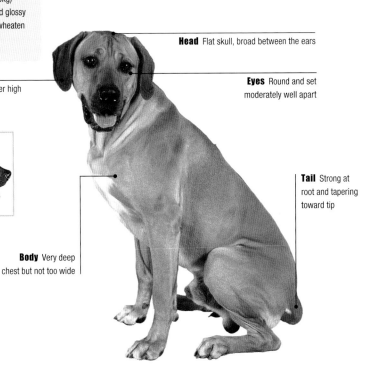

Head Flat skull, broad between the ears

Eyes Round and set moderately well apart

Ears Set rather high

Tail Strong at root and tapering toward tip

Body Very deep chest but not too wide

Grand Griffon Vendéen

The Griffons Vendéen are French sporting dogs that occur in a number of varieties, including the Grand and Petit Basset. The Grand is the largest and is reputedly the oldest of the varieties. It is thought to be a descendant of a white Saint Hubert Hound crossed with a tawny and white Italian bitch. The introduction of Nivernais Griffon and setter blood is said to have added stamina and endurance. Originally used for wolf hunting, the Grand is now used for wild boar.

The Grand Griffon Vendéen is an intelligent dog that makes a good family pet as well as a hunter. It is independent and loves to wander, so all escape routes should be sealed. It requires considerable exercise, and needs regular grooming with brush and comb.

Pedigree points

Recognized AKC, ANKC, CKC, FCI, KC(GB), KUSA

Height 24–26 in (61–66cm)

Weight 66–77 lb (30–35kg)

Coat Rough, long, and harsh to the touch, never silky or woolly, with a thick undercoat

Color Solid fawn or hare; white with red, fawn, gray, or black markings; bicolor or tricolor

Eyes Dark, without white, and with a kindly expression

Head Domed

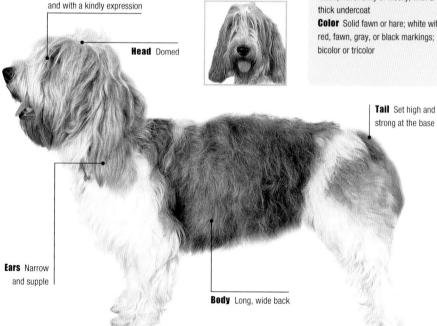

Tail Set high and strong at the base

Ears Narrow and supple

Body Long, wide back

Care requirements

1 **2** 3 4

1 **2** 3 4

1 2 3 4

1 **2** 3 4

Pedigree points

Recognized AKC, ANKC, CKC, FCI, KC(GB), KUSA
Height 13½–15 in (34–38cm)
Weight 25–35 lb (1.5–15.5kg)
Coat Rough, long, and harsh to the touch, never silky or woolly, with a thick undercoat
Color Solid fawn or hare; white with red, fawn, gray, or black markings; bicolor or tricolor

Petit Basset Griffon Vendéen

The Petit Basset Griffon Vendéen is a short-legged, rough-coated hound, developed in the Vendée district of south-west France. It was bred down from the Grand Griffon Vendéen. The Petit Basset Griffon Vendéen has been described as a miniature Basset reduced proportionately in size while retaining all its qualities—a passion for hunting, fearlessness in the densest coverts, and vigor. It is now used for hunting hare and rabbit, but can also manage larger game. It works very well in thick undergrowth.

This most attractive animal makes a good family pet provided that it receives plenty of exercise. It needs little grooming and considers humans its friends.

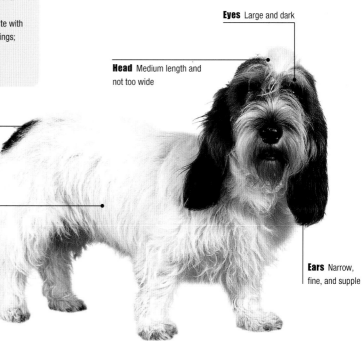

Eyes Large and dark

Head Medium length and not too wide

Tail Medium length, set high, and strong at the base

Body Deep chest with a prominent sternum

Ears Narrow, fine, and supple

Swiss Hounds

The scenthounds of Switzerland include the Swiss Hound, the Bernese Hound, and Lucernese Hound. There are also short-legged versions, produced by crossing the Dachshund with the full-size versions to produce specialized hunters for certain types of terrain. All three hounds are very similar in abilities, character, and appearance, except for color of coat. They have keen noses, great powers of endurance, and will work over any terrain. They make excellent tracking dogs and are used to hunt a variety of game, including hare, fox, and deer.

Swiss Hounds are calm companions but have strong hunting instincts and are powerfully built, and so are not suitable as household pets. They need a lot of exercise, and should be groomed with a hound glove, and a slicker for the rough-coated varieties.

Care requirements

4	3	2	1	🐕
4	3	2	1	🥣
4	3	2	1	🪮
4	3	2	1	🏠

Pedigree points

Recognized FCI
Height *Minimum:* 17½ in (44.5cm)
Generally: 18–22 in (45.5–56cm)
Short-legged varieties: 12–15 in (30–37.5cm)
Coat *Swiss & Bernese:* rough, wiry, with a thick undercoat *Lucernese:* short and very dense
Color *Swiss:* white with orange markings *Bernese:* white, black, with strong tan markings *Lucernese:* white with gray or blue speckling and broad dark or black markings

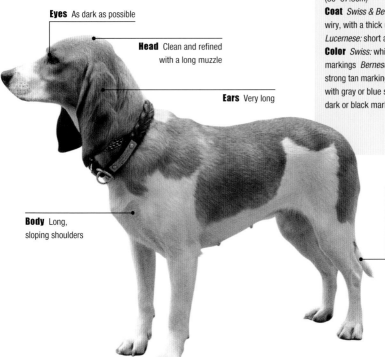

Eyes As dark as possible

Head Clean and refined with a long muzzle

Ears Very long

Tail Tapering

Body Long, sloping shoulders

Jura Hounds

There are two varieties of Jura Hound, the Bruno and the Saint Hubert. Both are native to the Jura mountains area in western Switzerland and have a similar origin to the other Swiss Hounds. However, they are closer in appearance to the Saint Hubert Bloodhound, particularly the Saint Hubert Jura, which has a heavier head, larger ears, and more pronounced folds of skin on the chin and neck than the Bruno. There are also short-legged versions. Enthusiastic hunters, Jura Hounds are used mainly against hare and can cope with any type of terrain.

The Bruno and Saint Hubert Jura Hounds are gentle, affectionate dogs that make excellent hunting companions, but have strong hunting instincts and are not really suited to life as a household pet. They need plenty of exercise and grooming with a hound glove.

Care requirements

1	2	3	4
1	2	3	4
1	2	3	4
1	2	3	4

Pedigree points

Recognized FCI
Height *Minimum:* 17½ in (44.5cm)
Generally: 18–22 in (45.5–56cm)
Coat Short
Color Yellowish or reddish brown, with or without large black saddle; black with tan markings over eyes, on cheeks, and on underparts of body; may have white mark on chest

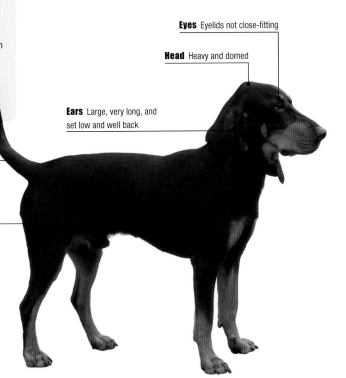

Eyes Eyelids not close-fitting

Head Heavy and domed

Ears Large, very long, and set low and well back

Tail Tapering

Body Medium-sized

Basset Hound

In common with members of the Greyhound family, Basset-type dogs were depicted on the tombs of the ancient Egyptians and so have obviously existed for a long time. However, the Basset Hound is fairly recent, having been developed in Britain from the late 1800s. It was bred from the French Basset Artésien Normand crossed with the Bloodhound to produce a slow but sure dog that was used in tracking rabbits and hare.

The Basset Hound is now mainly kept as a companion, pet, and show dog. It is a lovable animal that gets on well with children, but needs lots of exercise. Sweet-voiced and a superb tracker, it also has a propensity to wander, and fencing is essential if you own a Basset. The breed requires daily grooming with a hound glove.

Care requirements

4	3	2	1	🐕
4	3	2	1	🥣
4	3	2	1	🪮
4	3	2	1	🏠

Pedigree points

Recognized AKC, ANKC, CKC, FCI, KC(GB), KUSA

Height 13–14 in (33–35cm)

Weight 40–60 lb (18.1–27.2kg)

Coat Hard, smooth, short, and dense

Color Generally black, white, and tan (tricolor) or lemon and white (bicolor), but any recognized hound color acceptable

Eyes Lozenge-shaped

Head Domed, with some stop and prominent occipital bone

Ears Set low

Body Long and deep throughout length

Tail Well-set

Beagle

This small hound has existed in Britain at least since the reign of King Henry VIII. His daughter Elizabeth I kept numerous Beagles, some of which were so small they could be put in one's pocket and so became known as Pocket Beagles (now extinct). The breed is often known as the "singing Beagle" but is not noisy indoors, reserving its voice for the chase. In Britain it is adept at hunting hare and wild rabbit, and it has been used against wild pig and deer in Scandinavia, and the cottontail rabbit in the US.

This affectionate dog is usually long-lived and good with children. It makes a fine show dog, and is a good choice of family pet for those who do not demand exemplary behavior. In common with other hounds, it will take advantage of an open gate. Its weatherproof coat requires little or no attention, and the Beagle needs only average exercise when kept as a pet.

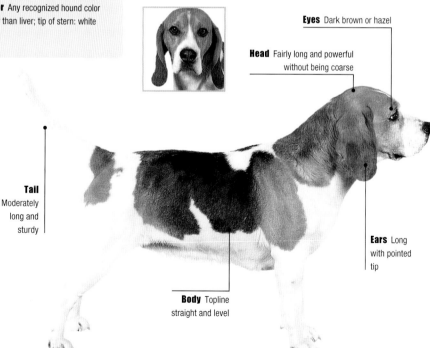

Eyes Dark brown or hazel

Head Fairly long and powerful without being coarse

Tail Moderately long and sturdy

Ears Long with pointed tip

Body Topline straight and level

Tawny Brittany Basset

The Tawny Brittany Basset or, as it is more commonly known, the Basset Fauve de Bretagne, originated in Brittany, north-west France. It was developed from the Basset Griffon Vendéen and other short-legged bassets to track over moorland and other rough terrain, where it is fast and active. A pack of these first-rate fox hunters was maintained by Francis I of France in the 16th century, but by the mid-1800s the type had become all but extinct, possibly due to its somewhat headstrong temperament. Resembling a large, rough-haired Dachshund in appearance, this hound has large, pendulous ears, a rough close coat, and is described as being "dumpy overall."

This short-legged, wire-coated hound has courage and a good nose. It requires a generous amount of exercise but its rough coat needs little attention.

Care requirements

4	3	2	1
4	3	2	1
4	3	2	1
4	3	2	1

Pedigree points

Recognized AKC, FCI, KC(GB), KUSA
Height 13–17 in (33–43cm)
Coat Harsh and close
Color Golden, wheaten, or fawn; white spot on neck or chest permissible

Head Moderate-length skull

Eyes Dark and alert

Tail Thick at root and tapering toward the tip

Ears Thin and set at eye level

Body Chest quite wide and well let down

Care requirements

1 2 3 4

1 2 3 4

1 2 3 4

1 2 3 4

Pedigree points

Recognized AKC, FCI, KC(GB).
Height *Dog:* 25–28 in (63.5–70cm)
Bitch: 23½–25½ in (60–65cm)
Weight 71–77 lb (34.5–36kg)
Coat Short, smooth, weather-resistant, and somewhat coarse
Color White with black patches and extensive black ticking to give appearance of blue dog; tan markings on head

Great Gascony Blue

The Great Gascony Blue is famed for its ability to pick up a "cold" scent. It descends from the scenting dogs of pre-Roman times and the ancient Saint Hubert Hound. Developed by the Count of Foix, Gaston Phoebus, in the 14th century, it became a favorite of the French King Henry IV in the 16th century. Even though this aristocratic animal is taller and lighter than many other hounds, it is very strong and is possessed of great stamina and a strong, melodious voice. It excelled at hunting wolves, which it pursued to extinction.

The Great Gascony Blue has a calm and friendly temperament. It requires a great deal of exercise and is not a suitable housepet. It should be groomed regularly and the long ears checked frequently.

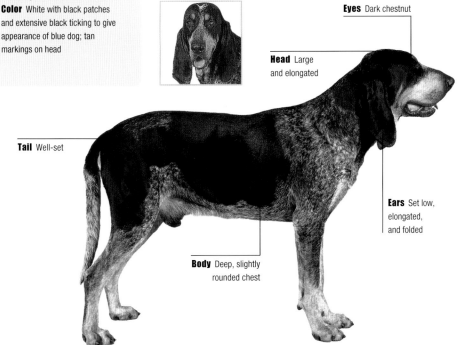

Eyes Dark chestnut

Head Large and elongated

Tail Well-set

Ears Set low, elongated, and folded

Body Deep, slightly rounded chest

Dachshund

There are six varieties of Dachshund: Smooth-haired, Long-haired, and Wire-haired, each occurring as both Standard and Miniature. The Dachshund derives from the oldest breeds of German hunting dogs, such as the Bibarhund, and existed as long ago as the 16th century. Originally there was only one variety, the Smooth-haired Dachshund. The Wire-haired was produced by introducing Dandie Dinmont and other terrier blood, while the Long-haired was formed by introducing the German Stöber, a gundog, to a Smooth-haired Dachshund and Spaniel cross.

Sporty and devoted, the Dachshund makes an excellent family pet and a good watchdog, with a surprisingly loud bark for its size. The Short-haired is easy to groom, requiring only daily attention with a hound glove and soft cloth. The Wire-haired and Long-haired should be brushed with a stiff-bristled brush and also combed.

Care requirements

4	3	2	1	
4	3	2	1	
4	3	2	1	
4	3	2	1	

Pedigree points

Recognized AKC, ANKC, CKC, FCI, KC (GB), KUSA

Weight *Standard:* 16–32 lb (7–14.5kg)
Miniature: under 11 lb (4.5kg)

Coat *Smooth-haired:* dense, short, and smooth *Long-haired:* soft, straight, and only slightly wavy *Wire-haired:* short, straight, and harsh, with a long undercoat

Color All colors but white are permissible; small patch on the chest permitted but not desirable; dappled dogs may include white but should be evenly marked all over

Smooth-haired Dachshund

The oldest of the Dachshund varieties, the Smooth-haired is a favorite in Britain and the United States.

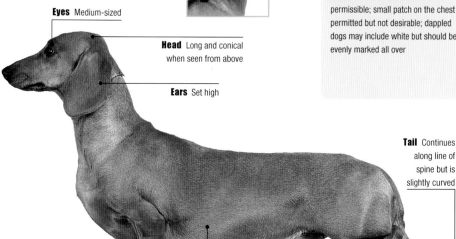

Eyes Medium-sized

Head Long and conical when seen from above

Ears Set high

Tail Continues along line of spine but is slightly curved

Body Long and full-muscled

Wire-haired grizzled

Wire-haired Dachshund

The Wire-haired Dachshund results from cross-mating with various terrier breeds.

Miniature Wire-haired tan

Miniature Long-haired black and tan

Long-haired Dachshund

Cross-breeding between the Smooth-haired and gundog types yielded the Long-haired Dachshund.

Long-haired tan

Greyhound

The Greyhound is arguably the purest breed on Earth, appearing to have changed little from dogs depicted on the tombs of Egyptian pharaohs. It also has the distinction of a mention in the Bible in the Book of Solomon. It is likely that the Greyhound found its way to Afghanistan, where its coat thickened to contend with the colder climate, and was then brought to Europe by the Celts. Possessing keen eyesight and capable of great speed, this sighthound was highly valued as a courser and, more recently, as a competitor on the racing track.

The Greyhound does have a propensity to chase anything that moves, but is also a gentle, faithful animal that is good with children. It needs a daily brushing and average but regular exercise on hard ground, and takes up relatively little space, having a liking for its own special corner.

Care requirements

4	3	2	1	🐕
4	3	2	1	🍽
4	3	2	1	🪮
4	3	2	1	🏠

Pedigree points

Recognized AKC, ANKC, CKC, FCI, KC(GB), KUSA
Height *Dog:* 28–30 in (71–76cm)
Bitch: 27–28 in (68–71cm)
Weight *Dog:* 65–70 lb (29.5–31.5kg)
Bitch: 60–65 lb (27–29.5kg)
Coat Fine and close
Color Black, white, red, blue, fawn, fallow brindle, or any of these colors broken with white

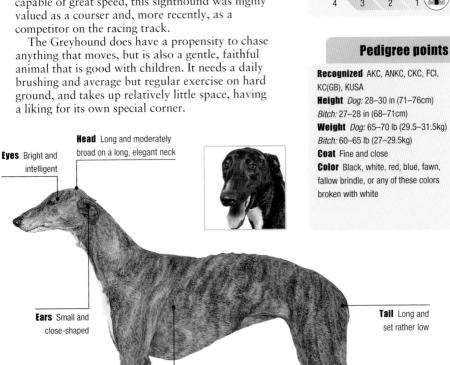

Eyes Bright and intelligent

Head Long and moderately broad on a long, elegant neck

Ears Small and close-shaped

Body Deep, capacious chest

Tail Long and set rather low

Whippet

The Whippet looks like a Greyhound in miniature, and the Greyhound undoubtedly played a part in its make-up. It is uncertain whether the Pharaoh Hound, as seems likely, or some other imported hound or terrier, was the other half of the cross. The Whippet was bred expressly as a racing dog, and is the fastest breed in the world. It has been timed at 8.4 seconds over a standard 150 yard (137m) straight course (36.52mph/58.76kmh).

The Whippet is a gentle dog that is good with children and makes a fine pet and show dog, and a splendid watchdog. While it can adapt to domestic life, this powerful runner needs plenty of exercise. Its short coat requires little other than a brush and rub-down, but it does mean that the dog is better housed indoors year round rather than kenneled outside.

Care requirements

1	2	3	4
1	2	3	4
1	2	3	4
1	2	3	4

Pedigree points

Recognized AKC, ANKC, CKC, FCI, KC(GB), KUSA
Height *Dog:* 18½–20 in (47–51cm)
Bitch: 17½–18½ in (44–47cm)
Weight 28 lb (12.5kg)
Coat Short, fine, and close
Color Any color or mixture of colors

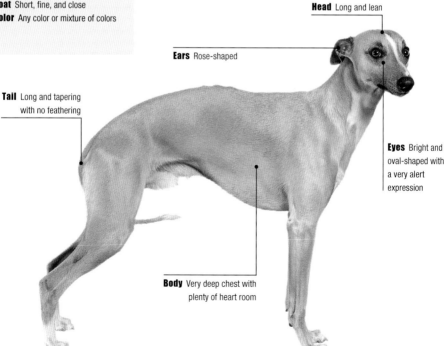

Head Long and lean

Ears Rose-shaped

Tail Long and tapering with no feathering

Eyes Bright and oval-shaped with a very alert expression

Body Very deep chest with plenty of heart room

Deerhound

One of the most ancient British breeds, the Deerhound may have arrived in Scotland with Phoenician traders about 3,000 years ago, and thereafter developed its thick, weather-resistant coat to combat the colder climate. The breed became a favorite of chieftains in the Scottish Highlands, hunting with them by day and gracing their baronial halls by night. Today, the Deerhound is used for coursing and draws good entries at dog shows.

Although gentle in the home, the breed needs careful training around livestock, for it can kill when its hunting instincts are roused. With its shaggy coat, it is no hardship for this breed to be kenneled outdoors—in fact, it does not like intense heat. It needs lots of exercise but the minimum of grooming—just the removal of stray hairs for showing.

Care requirements

4	3	2	1
4	3	2	1
4	3	2	1
4	3	2	1

Pedigree points

Recognized AKC, ANKC, CKC, FCI, KC(GB), KUSA
Height *Dog:* 30–32 in (76–80cm)
Bitch: at least 28 in (71cm)
Weight *Dog:* 85–110 lb (38–48.5kg)
Bitch: 75–95 lb (33.5–42.5kg)
Coat Shaggy but not overcoated
Color Dark blue gray and lighter grays; brindles and yellows; sandy red or red fawn with black points

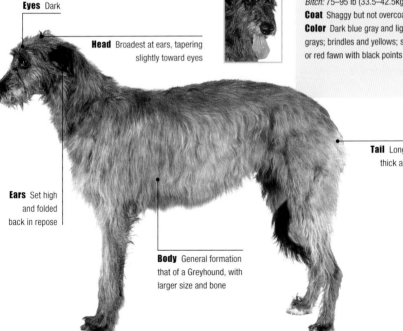

Eyes Dark

Head Broadest at ears, tapering slightly toward eyes

Tail Long and thick at root

Ears Set high and folded back in repose

Body General formation that of a Greyhound, with larger size and bone

Care requirements

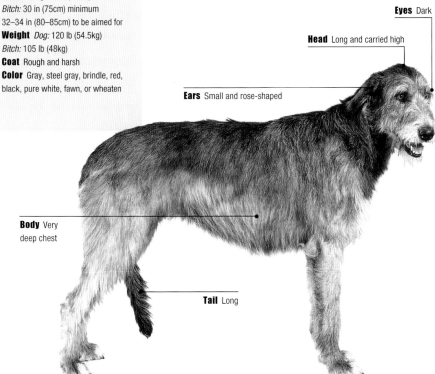

	1	2	3	4
	1	2	3	4
	1	2	3	4
	1	2	3	4

Pedigree points

Recognized AKC, ANKC, CKC, FCI, KC(GB), KUSA

Height *Dog:* 32 in (80cm) minimum
Bitch: 30 in (75cm) minimum
32–34 in (80–85cm) to be aimed for

Weight *Dog:* 120 lb (54.5kg)
Bitch: 105 lb (48kg)

Coat Rough and harsh

Color Gray, steel gray, brindle, red, black, pure white, fawn, or wheaten

Irish Wolfhound

The Irish Wolfhound is the tallest dog in the world, and the national dog of Ireland. Bred to kill wolves, it is thought to be descended from dogs brought by the Celts as they spread across Europe from Greece, which they invaded in about 279 BC, to Ireland.

The Irish Wolfhound is a breed that many people would choose to own if only their lifestyle and house size enabled them to. However, the Wolfhound does not require more exercise than average-sized breeds, and although it can be kenneled outdoors, it has a calm temperament, and many of these giants have a place by the fireside. The breed is popular in the show ring, and since it is exhibited in what is deemed a "natural state," brushing and the removal of straggly hairs are all the preparation that is required.

Eyes Dark

Head Long and carried high

Ears Small and rose-shaped

Body Very deep chest

Tail Long

Saluki

The Saluki is an ancient breed whose likeness appears on the tombs of Egyptian pharaohs. It takes its name either from the ancient city of Saluk in the Yemen or the town of Seleukia in the ancient Hellenic empire in Syria. It is also known as the Gazelle Hound, the Arab Gazelle Hound, the Eastern Greyhound, and the Persian Greyhound. The Saluki is esteemed by the Arabs, including the nomadic Bedouin, who prize it for its ability to keep pace with fleet-footed Arab horses and, paired with a falcon, to hunt gazelle.

This elegant, if somewhat aloof, breed is loyal and affectionate, and is sought both as a pet and show dog. It requires plenty of exercise, and care should be taken in the countryside that its hunting instincts are kept under control. The Saluki's coat should be groomed daily, using a soft brush and a hound glove.

Care requirements

4	3	2	1
4	3	2	1
4	3	2	1
4	3	2	1

Pedigree points

Recognized AKC, ANKC, CKC, FCI, KC(GB), KUSA
Height *Dog:* 23–28 in (58.5–71cm)
Bitch: smaller
Coat Smooth and silky in texture
Color White, cream, fawn, golden red, grizzle, silver grizzle, deer grizzle, tricolor (white, black, and tan), or variations of these colors

Eyes Dark to hazel

Head Long and narrow

Ears Long, mobile, and not set too low

Tail Set low from long, gently sloping pelvis

Body Fairly broad back and strong hip bones set wide apart

Borzoi

The Borzoi or Russian Wolfhound was used in Russia from the 17th century for wolf hunting and coursing, a sport of the tsars and noblemen. The Borzoi tracked the wolf, when it was beaten from cover, but did not kill it. The dog's task was to grab the wolf by the neck and throw it, whereupon it would be finished off with a blow from a dagger.

The Borzoi is an elegant, intelligent, and faithful, albeit somewhat aloof, pet and a reasonably popular show dog. It is not ideally suited to being a child's pet as it does not take kindly to teasing. It requires a considerable amount of space and exercise, and care must be taken that it does not worry livestock. Its coat needs surprisingly little attention.

Care requirements

	1	2	3	4
🐕	1	2	3	4
🥣	1	2	3	4
🪮	1	2	3	4
🏠	1	2	3	4

Pedigree points

Recognized AKC, ANKC, CKC, FCI, KC(GB), KUSA
Height *Dog:* 29 in (74cm)
Bitch: 27 in (68cm)
Weight *Dog:* 75–105 lb (33.5–65kg)
Bitch: 60–85 lb (27.5–38.5kg)
Coat Silky, flat, and wavy or rather curly; never woolly
Color Any color acceptable

Eyes Dark with intelligent, alert expression

Head Long, lean, and in proportion to overall size

Tail Long and set rather low

Ears Small, pointed, and delicate

Body Deep, narrow chest

Elkhound

The Gray Norwegian Elkhound has probably existed in its native Scandinavia for millennia. Archeologists have discovered bones of similar dogs dating back to 5000–4000 BC. Its task was to seek an elk and hold it at bay until its master moved in for the kill. There is also a Miniature Elkhound and a Black Elkhound, the latter being little known outside its native Norway.

Although somewhat willful in youth, the Elkhound is generally a good-natured household pet that has no doggie odor and is reliable with children. It requires daily brushing and combing, and plenty of exercise.

Care requirements

4	3	2	1	🐕
4	3	2	1	🥣
4	3	2	1	🖌
4	3	2	1	🏠

Pedigree points

Recognized AKC, ANKC, CKC, FCI, KC(GB), KUSA
Height *Dog:* 20½ in (52cm)
Bitch: 19½ in (49cm)
Weight *Dog:* 50 lb (23kg)
Bitch: 43 lb (20kg)
Coat Close, abundant, and weather-resistant; outer coat coarse and straight, undercoat soft and woolly
Color Various shades of gray with black tips to hairs on outer coat; lighter on chest, stomach, legs, underside of tail, buttocks, and in a harness mark

Eyes Slightly oval

Head Wedge-shaped

Ears Set high

Tail Strong and set high

Body Powerful

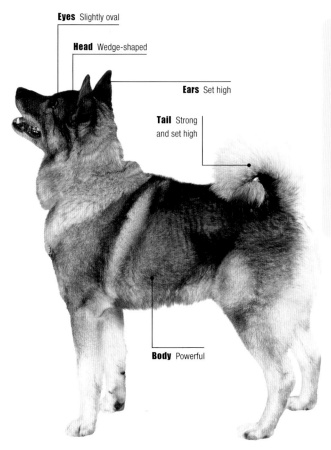

Care requirements

1 2 3 4

1 2 3 4

1 2 3 4

1 2 3 4

Pedigree points

Recognized AKC, ANKC, CKC, FCI, KC(GB), KUSA
Height *Dog:* 27 in (68cm)
Bitch: 25 in (63cm)
Weight *Dog:* 60 lb (27kg)
Bitch: 50 lb (22.5kg)
Coat Long and fine
Color All colors acceptable

Afghan Hound

This member of the Greyhound family, possibly related to the Saluki, is said by legend to have been one of the animals taken aboard Noah's Ark. Its ancestors somehow found their way from their original home Persia (Iran) to Afghanistan, where the breed developed its long, shaggy coat to withstand the harsh climatic conditions. Its speed and stamina meant that it was used to hunt leopards, wolves, and jackals. It has since become a popular show dog and has been utilized in the growing sport of Afghan racing.

The Afghan is an elegant and affectionate dog that is generally good natured but does not tolerate teasing. It is intelligent, somewhat aloof, and requires plenty of exercise. The coat should be groomed with an air-cushioned brush and will soon become matted if it is not given sufficient and regular attention.

Head Long and not too narrow

Eyes Preferably dark, but golden and not debarred

Ears Set low and well back

Tail Not too short

Body Moderately long, level back

Terriers

Bull Terrier

Some people consider this breed the picture of ugliness, while others have only admiration for the Bull Terrier, which is described somewhat poetically in its standard as "the gladiator of the canine race." The Bull Terrier began life as a fighting dog and was the result of crossing an Old English Bulldog with a terrier. The first Bull Terriers were said to have closely resembled the Staffordshire Bull Terrier, but then Dalmatian and possibly other blood was introduced.

Despite its fierce appearance and strength, the Bull Terrier makes a faithful and devoted pet. The bitch, in particular, is utterly reliable with children. However, this breed is too strong for other than the able bodied to handle, and needs careful training. Its short, flat coat is easy to look after.

Care requirements

4	3	2	1
4	3	2	1
4	3	2	1
4	3	2	1

Pedigree points

Recognized AKC, ANKC, CKC, FCI, KC(GB), KUSA
Height 21–22 in (52.5–55cm)
Weight 52–62 lb (23.5–28kg)
Coat Short and flat
Color White: pure white coat; coloreds: brindle preferred; black, red, fawn, or tricolor acceptable

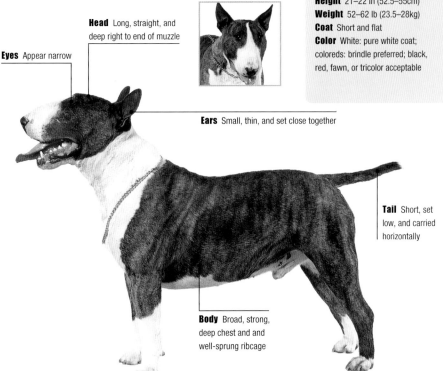

Head Long, straight, and deep right to end of muzzle

Eyes Appear narrow

Ears Small, thin, and set close together

Tail Short, set low, and carried horizontally

Body Broad, strong, deep chest and and well-sprung ribcage

Care requirements

	1	2	3	4
	1	2	3	4
	1	2	3	4
	1	2	3	4

Pedigree points

Recognized AKC, ANKC, CKC, FCI, KC(GB), KUSA
Height 10–14 in (25–35.5cm)
Weight 10–40 lb (4.5–18kg)
Coat Short, flat, with a fine gloss
Color Pure white, black, brindle, red, fawn, or tricolor acceptable

Miniature Bull Terrier

This dog is a smaller replica of the Bull Terrier and shares the same breed standard apart from height. Bull Terriers weighing as little as 10 lb (4.5kg) were recorded early in the breed's history, but it was not until 1939 that the Miniature was given a separate breed register by the Kennel Club in Britain. It has never been very popular and few specimens are seen in the show ring.

This loving and companionable little dog has the same characteristics as its larger relative, making an excellent pet and being generally good with children. It requires daily brushing and plenty of exercise.

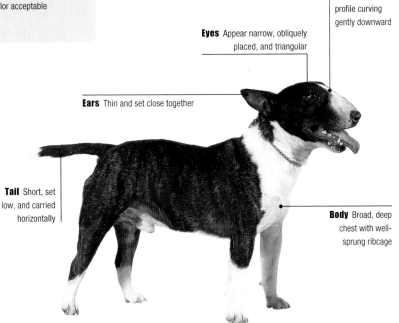

Head Long, strong, and deep, with profile curving gently downward

Eyes Appear narrow, obliquely placed, and triangular

Ears Thin and set close together

Tail Short, set low, and carried horizontally

Body Broad, deep chest with well-sprung ribcage

Staffordshire Bull Terrier

The Staffordshire Bull Terrier should not be confused with the American Staffordshire Terrier, or Pit Bull, which has been developed along quite different lines. The lovable Staffordshire or Staffy has a bloody history. It derived from the crossing of an Old English Bulldog and a terrier, most likely the extinct Black and Tan, at a time when bull-baiting and dog fighting were two of the most popular "sports" in Britain. The resultant dogs had the ideal attributes for combat: the strength and tenacity of a bulldog coupled with the agility and quick wits of a terrier. When bull-baiting and, thereafter, dog fighting were outlawed in Britain, the Staffy was developed along gentler lines as a companion dog.

The Staffy is one of the most popular pets and show dogs. It makes a fine household dog as well as guard, being an affectionate and game companion that adores children. However, it is not averse to having a fight with its fellows, usually emerging the victor, and so it is sensible to keep it on the leash while out walking. This totally reliable, smooth-coated dog is easy to look after, requiring little other than regular brushing.

Heavily built of almost solid muscle, the Staffordshire Bull Terrier still resembles its bulldog/terrier ancestors. Originally bred as a fighting dog, it has now gained widespread popularity as a family pet.

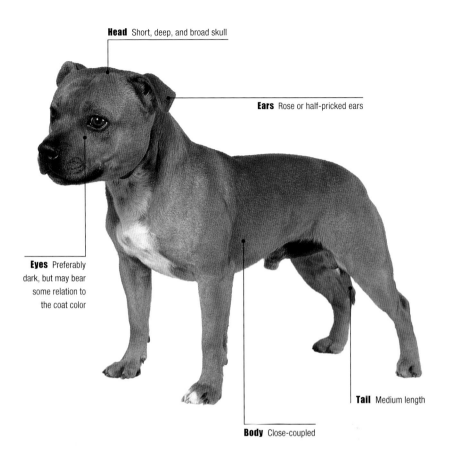

Head Short, deep, and broad skull

Ears Rose or half-pricked ears

Eyes Preferably dark, but may bear some relation to the coat color

Tail Medium length

Body Close-coupled

Pedigree points

Recognized AKC, ANKC, CKC, FCI, KC(GB), KUSA
Height 14–16 in (35.5–40.5cm)
Weight *Dog:* 28–38 lb (12.5–17kg)
Bitch: 24–34 lb (11–15.5kg)
Coat Smooth, short, and dense
Color Red, fawn, white, black, or blue, or any one of these colors with white; any shade of brindle, or any shade of brindle with white

Care requirements

	1	2	3	4
	1	2	3	4
	1	2	3	4
	1	2	3	4

Airedale Terrier

The Airedale is the king of the terriers, being the largest member of the terrier group. The Airedale was named after the Valley of Aire in Yorkshire, England. It was the progeny of a working terrier probably crossed with the Otterhound. An expert ratter and duck-catcher, the Airedale can also be trained to the gun and is a splendid guard. It has undertaken a multitude of tasks, ranging from service in both the British and Russian armies to acting as messenger for the Red Cross and as a railway police patrol dog.

The multipurpose Airedale is a good choice for the terrier devotee who wants a bigger dog. As a family pet, it is good with children, extremely loyal, and despite its size, seems to adapt well to fairly cramped conditions, provided that it has plenty of exercise. It will, however, need to be hand stripped twice a year, if it is the intention to exhibit.

Care requirements

4 3 2 1
4 3 2 1
4 3 2 1
4 3 2 1

Pedigree points

Recognized AKC, ANKC, CKC, FCI, KC(GB), KUSA
Height *Dog:* 23–24 in (58–61cm)
Bitch: 22–23 in (56–59cm)
Weight 44 lb (20kg)
Coat Hard, dense, and wiry
Color Black or grizzle body saddle, top of neck, and top surface of tail; all other parts tan; ears often a darker tan, and shading may occur around neck and side of skull; a few white hairs between forelegs are acceptable

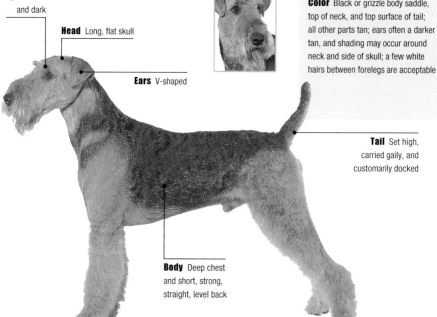

Eyes small and dark

Head Long, flat skull

Ears V-shaped

Tail Set high, carried gaily, and customarily docked

Body Deep chest and short, strong, straight, level back

Bedlington Terrier

The Bedlington Terrier looks like a shorn lamb with its distinctive thick, linty coat standing well out from the skin. This breed was once a favorite with poachers and is still known by some as the Gypsy Dog. It is believed that the Greyhound or Whippet played a part in its ancestry and possibly also the Dandie Dinmont Terrier. The Bedlington probably originated in Northumberland, in the north of England.

The Bedlington is a true terrier: lovable, full of fun, and a terror when its temper is provoked. It is, however, easy to train and usually adores children. It does not need a great deal of space, enjoys average exercise, and while its coat needs regular trimming, a good grooming every day using a stiff brush will normally keep it tidy.

Care requirements

1 **2** 3 4

1 **2** 3 4

1 **2** 3 4

1 **2** 3 4

Pedigree points

Recognized AKC, ANKC, CKC, FCI, KC(GB), KUSA

Height *Dog:* 16–17½ in (40.5–44cm) *Bitch:* 15–16½ in (37.5–41cm)

Weight 18–22 lb (8–10.5kg)

Coat Thick and linty

Color Blue, liver, or sandy, with or without tan; darker pigment to be encouraged; blues, and blue and tans, must have black noses; livers and sandies must have brown noses

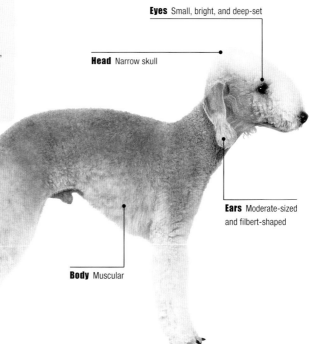

Eyes Small, bright, and deep-set

Head Narrow skull

Tail Moderate length, thick at root, and tapering to a point

Ears Moderate-sized and filbert-shaped

Body Muscular

Smooth Fox Terrier

The Smooth Fox Terrier started life as a stable dog, its job being to hunt vermin. It probably descends from terriers in the English counties of Cheshire and Shropshire with some beagle blood added. Terriers have hunted foxes, badgers, and vermin for centuries. When foxhunting from horseback became popular among the British gentry in the 1800s, a Fox Terrier was carried in a saddle bag, ready to be released in order to flush out the fox from its lair. The Industrial Revolution only increased the breed's popularity—in towns as ratters and in the country for foxhunts.

Fox Terriers are affectionate, trainable, and make the ideal child's companion for rabbiting. The Smooth needs daily grooming with a stiff brush, and trimming and chalking before a show.

Care requirements

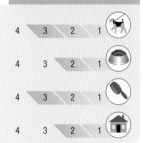

Pedigree points

Recognized AKC, ANKC, CKC, FCI, KC(GB), KUSA
Height *Dog:* 15½ in (39cm)
Bitch: slightly less
Weight 16–18 lb (7–8kg)
Coat Straight, flat, and smooth
Color All white; white with tan or black markings, with white predominant; brindle, red, or liver markings highly undesirable

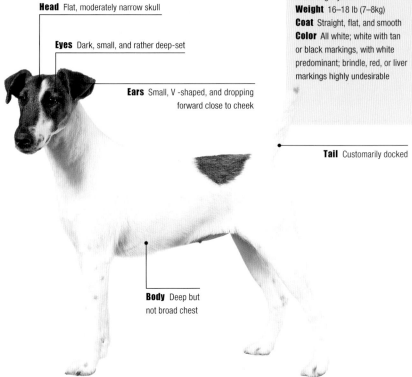

Head Flat, moderately narrow skull

Eyes Dark, small, and rather deep-set

Ears Small, V-shaped, and dropping forward close to cheek

Tail Customarily docked

Body Deep but not broad chest

Wire Fox Terrier

🐕	1	2	3	4
🥣	1	2	3	4
🪮	1	2	3	4
🏠	1	2	3	4

Pedigree points

Recognized AKC, ANKC, CKC, FCI, KC(GB), KUSA
Height *Dog:* 15½ in (39cm)
Bitch: slightly less
Weight 16–18 lb (7–8kg)
Coat Dense and very wiry
Color White should predominate with black or tan markings; brindle, red, liver, or slate-blue markings undesirable

The Wire Fox Terrier closely resembles the Smooth Fox Terrier, except for the wire coat. The Smooth and the Wire were originally considered one breed with two varieties, but are now divided into two distinct breeds. The early ancestors of the Wire were probably the old rough-coated Black and Tan Terriers of the coal-mining areas of Durham and Derbyshire in England, and in Wales. Later they were crossed with the Smooth Fox Terrier to improve the head and gain the white color. Crossbreeding of the two varieties ceased around 1900.

The Wire is more popular than its smooth-coated relative. Usually good tempered and reliable with older children, the Wire Fox Terrier is always ready for fun. The Wire needs to be hand-stripped three times a year, and to be groomed regularly.

Head Topline of skull almost flat

Eyes Dark and full of fire and intelligence

Ears Small, V-shaped, and moderately thick

Tail Customarily docked

Body Short, strong, level back

Irish Terrier

The Irish or Irish Red Terrier is reminiscent of a small Airedale Terrier, except for its fiery coat color. The Irish claim that this, their national terrier, is a smaller version of the Irish Wolfhound and has been in existence in Ireland for centuries. However, the first official record of it did not occur until 1875. It seems more likely that the Irish Terrier is a descendant of wire-haired Black and Tan Terriers, whose job was to repel vermin and hunt some 200 years ago. A study of the very similar Welsh and Lakeland Terriers supports this suggestion. In the case of the Irish, the blood of a Wheaten Terrier may also have been introduced.

The attractive Irish is an expert ratter and has been trained to the gun with success. It also makes an affectionate pet. Its coat should be stripped two or three times a year, and it should be groomed regularly.

Care requirements

4	3	2	1	🐕
4	3	2	1	🥣
4	3	2	1	🧴
4	3	2	1	🏠

Pedigree points

Recognized AKC, ANKC, CKC, FCI, KC(GB), KUSA
Height 18 in (46cm)
Weight 25–27 lb (11.5–12kg)
Coat Harsh and wiry
Color Whole-colored, preferably red, red wheaten, or yellow-red; small amount of white on chest acceptable; white on feet or any black shading highly undesirable

Head Long, flat, and narrow between ears

Ears Small and V-shaped

Eyes Small, dark, and not prominent

Tail Deep, muscular, and customarily docked

Body Deep, muscular chest, but not full or wide

Kerry Blue Terrier

Care requirements

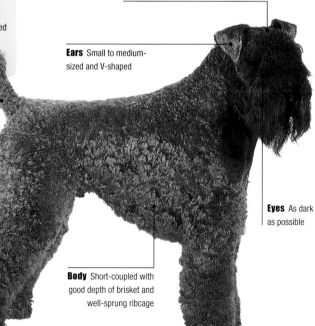

- 1 2 3 4
- 1 2 3 4
- 1 2 3 4
- 1 2 3 4

Pedigree points

Recognized AKC, ANKC, CKC, FCI, KC(GB), KUSA
Height *Dog:* 18–19½ in (45–49cm)
Bitch: 17½–19 in (44–47.5cm)
Weight 33–40 lb (15–18kg)
Coat Soft, spiky, plentiful, and wavy
Color Any shade of blue, with or without black points; a small white patch on chest should not be penalized

The Kerry Blue Terrier originated in County Kerry, south-western Ireland. An excellent sporting dog and fine swimmer, it was used there to hunt badgers, foxes, and otters. Its ancestors are thought to have included the Irish, Bedlington, and Bull Terriers. As with the Irish Terrier, there is a school of thought that the Irish Wolfhound also contributed to its make-up.

Although it began life as a sporting dog, the Kerry Blue is now mainly kept as a pet. It is good with children, but it may display a fierce temper against dogs or other pets when roused, and so, if you own a fiery Kerry, you would be wise to insure yourself against other people's veterinary bills. The Kerry is not the easiest dog to prepare for the show ring, requiring knowledgeable trimming. It needs daily grooming with a stiff brush and metal-toothed comb.

Head Long with flat skull and full foreface

Ears Small to medium-sized and V-shaped

Tail Set high, carried erect, and customarily docked

Eyes As dark as possible

Body Short-coupled with good depth of brisket and well-sprung ribcage

Terriers

Glen of Imaal Terrier

This short-legged terrier derives from the Glen of Imaal in County Wicklow, Ireland, where it has existed for a very long time. It was used to dispel vermin, including fox and badger, and in dog fights. Badger hunting and dog fighting are now illegal, but its other skills continue to be employed. The Glen of Imaal Terrier received official breed recognition in its own country in 1933, but remains little known outside its native Ireland.

The Glen of Imaal is now kept mainly as a family pet and/or working terrier on Irish farms and small holdings. It is affectionate, brave, good with children, and very playful. Maintaining its charming, shaggy dog appearance requires only a good daily brushing.

Care requirements

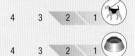

4	3	2	1	🐕
4	3	2	1	🥣
4	3	2	1	🪮
4	3	2	1	🏠

Pedigree points

Recognized ANKC, FCI, KC(GB), KUSA
Height 14 in (35.5cm)
Weight 35 lb (15.7kg)
Coat Medium length and harsh, with a soft undercoat
Color All shades of blue, brindle, or wheaten

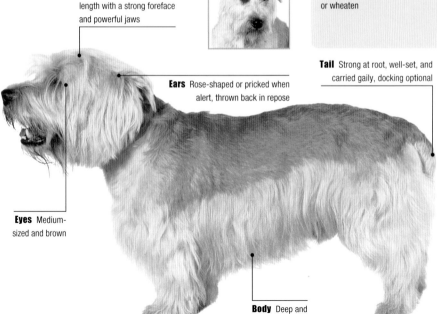

Head Good width and fair length with a strong foreface and powerful jaws

Tail Strong at root, well-set, and carried gaily, docking optional

Ears Rose-shaped or pricked when alert, thrown back in repose

Eyes Medium-sized and brown

Body Deep and medium length

Care requirements

🐕 1 2 3 4

🥣 1 2 3 4

🪮 1 2 3 4

🏠 1 2 3 4

Pedigree points

Recognized AKC, ANKC, CKC, FCI, KC(GB), KUSA
Height *Dog:* 18–19½ in (45.5–49.5cm) *Bitch:* slightly less
Weight 35–45 lb (15.5–20kg)
Coat Soft and silky
Color A good, clear wheaten, the shade of ripening wheat; white and red equally objectionable; dark shading on ears not untypical

Soft-coated Wheaten Terrier

One of the oldest native dog breeds of Ireland, the Soft-coated Wheaten Terrier is believed to be a progenitor of the Irish and Kerry Blue Terriers. It is said that a blue dog swam ashore from a ship wrecked in Tralee Bay, Ireland, around 180 years ago. This dog mated with the native Wheaten and the result of the union was the Kerry Blue Terrier. The Soft-coated Wheaten was developed as a farm dog to hunt rabbits, rats, and other prey.

Despite being bred as a farmyard dog, the Soft-coated Wheaten does best when housed indoors as a family pet. It is gentle and devoted, and generally loves children. It revels in plenty of exercise, and the coat should be groomed regularly using a medium-toothed metal comb and a wire brush.

Eyes Clear, bright, and dark hazel

Head Moderately long with flat skull

Ears V-shaped

Tail Customarily docked

Body Compact

Lakeland Terrier

The Lakeland Terrier comes from the Lake District in the old English county of Cumberland. It was developed with the aim of protecting lambs from foxes. To meet this aim, there were various terrier crossings, and it is thought that the Border, the Bedlington, and the Dandie Dinmont Terriers, and probably later the Fox Terrier, all contributed. The result is a practical and courageous working animal, resembling an Airedale Terrier in miniature, which is small enough to follow prey underground.

The Lakeland Terrier has retained its sporting instincts yet makes an excellent housepet, being a smart little guard and good with children. However, it is a lively dog, needing a fair amount of exercise. Its coat requires daily brushing, and if it is the intention to exhibit, will have to be stripped three times a year.

Care requirements

4	3	2	1
4	3	2	1
4	3	2	1
4	3	2	1

Pedigree points

Recognized AKC, ANKC, CKC, FCI, KC(GB), KUSA

Height 14½ in (37cm)

Weight *Dog:* 17 lb (7.5kg)
Bitch: 15 lb (7kg)

Coat Dense and harsh, with weather-resistant undercoat

Color Black and tan, blue and tan, red, wheaten, red grizzle, liver, blue, or black; mahogany or deep tan not typical; small tips of white on feet and chest undesirable but permissible

Tail Customarily docked

Head Flat skull

Ears Moderately small

Eyes Refined and dark or hazel

Body Reasonably narrow chest

Manchester Terrier

Care requirements

1 **2** 3 4

1 **2** 3 4

1 2 3 4

1 **2** 3 4

Pedigree points

Recognized AKC, ANKC, CKC, FCI, KC(GB). KUSA
Height *Dog:* 16 in (40.5cm)
Bitch: 15 in (38cm)
Weight 12–22 lb (5.5–10kg)
Coat Close, smooth, short, and glossy
Color Jet black and rich tan

The ancestors of the Manchester Terrier were sporting terriers that would demolish rats in a pit for the amusement of spectators in the mid-19th century. This sport was popular among poorer people in areas such as the city of Manchester in northern England. The Manchester Terrier appears to descend from the now extinct White English Terrier, with the addition of Dachshund, Whippet, and King Charles Spaniel blood. The Doberman and Italian Greyhound contributed to the Manchester's shiny coat and coloring, and the latter to its slightly arched back.

The long-lived Manchester Terrier tends to be a one-person animal. It also makes a good family pet, and is suited to a town or country existence. The only grooming required is a daily brush and rub-down.

Head Long, flat, narrow skull

Eyes Small, dark, and sparkling

Tail Set where arch of back ends

Ears Small and V-shaped

Body Narrow, deep chest

Parson Jack Russell Terrier

The Parson Jack Russell Terrier takes its name from a sporting parson, Jack Russell, who lived in the county of Devon, England, in the 1800s. He was a horseman, a terrier judge, and one of the early members of the British Kennel Club. Parson Russell developed this strain of terriers from various early types of Wire Fox Terrier to obtain dogs that would run with hounds and bolt the fox from its lair. Their coat may be either rough and broken, or smooth.

The Parson Jack Russell is still an extremely good working terrier, and has become enormously popular as a household pet. It can be somewhat excitable and is best suited to being the companion of an active child. It requires little grooming.

Care requirements

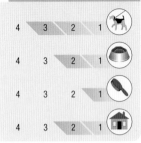

4	3	2	1
4	3	2	1
4	3	2	1
4	3	2	1

Pedigree points

Recognized ANKC, FCI, KC(GB), KUSA
Height *Dog:* 13–14 in (33–35cm)
Bitch: 12–13 in (30–33cm)
Coat Smooth, or rough and broken
Color Entirely white or with tan, lemon, or black markings, preferably confined to head and root of tail

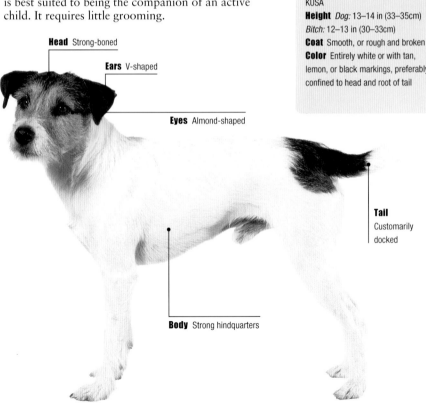

Head Strong-boned

Ears V-shaped

Eyes Almond-shaped

Tail Customarily docked

Body Strong hindquarters

Border Terrier

Care requirements

	1	2	3	4
🐕	1	2	3	4
🥣	1	2	3	4
🖌	1	2	3	4
🏠	1	2	3	4

Pedigree points

Recognized AKC, ANKC, CKC, FCI, KC(GB), KUSA
Height 10 in (25cm)
Weight *Dog:* 13–15½ lb (6–7kg)
Bitch: 11½–14 lb (5–6.5kg)
Coat Harsh and dense with close undercoat
Color Red, wheaten, grizzle and tan, or blue and tan

This attractive, tough little dog derives from the Border country, the area around the boundary between England and Scotland, and is probably still seen in its largest numbers there. The Border Terrier was bred in the middle of the 19th century to be higher on the leg than most terriers of the same general size, which enabled it to run with hounds and yet be small enough to bolt the fox from its lair.

The smallest of the working terriers, the Border makes a first-class pet. It usually loves all children, is long lived, will literally walk its owners off their feet, and is a good watchdog. It still retains all its hunting instincts and will happily take off on an expedition alone if allowed to roam unsupervised. It requires little routine grooming, and only a slight tidying up before exhibiting.

Head Moderately broad and flat skull

Eyes Dark with keen expression

Ears Small and V-shaped

Tail Moderately short

Body Deep, narrow, and fairly long

Welsh Terrier

The Welsh Terrier resembles very closely both the Lakeland Terrier and the larger Airedale Terrier. Like another similar terrier, the Irish, the Welsh Terrier is of Celtic origin. Two strains of it were evolved by the Welsh, a Celtic strain using a coarse-haired Black and Tan Terrier and an English strain using an Airedale and a Fox Terrier cross, and appeared as a distinct breed in the late 18th century. The English strain is said to have died out. These terriers were originally popular for hunting badger, fox, and otter.

The Welsh Terrier is energetic, affectionate, and good with children. It enjoys plenty of exercise and will need to have its coat stripped at least twice a year, if it is the intention to exhibit. Many owners of pet Welsh Terriers have their dog's coat clipped.

Care requirements

4   3   2   1

4   3   2   1

4   3   2   1

4   3   2   1

Pedigree points

Recognized AKC, ANKC, CKC, FCI, KC(GB), KUSA
Height 15½ in (39cm) maximum
Weight 20–21 lb (9–9.5kg)
Coat Abundant, wiry, hard, and close
Color Black and tan for preference; also black, grizzle, and tan; free from black penciling on toes; black below hocks most undesirable

Eyes Small, dark, and well-set

Head Flat and moderately wide between ears

Ears V-shaped and carried forward

Tail Well-set and customarily docked

Body Short, well-ribbed, with long, muscular legs

Cairn Terrier

Care requirements

1 **2** 3 4

1 **2** 3 4

1 2 3 4

1 2 3 4

Pedigree points

Recognized AKC, ANKC, CKC, FCI, KC(GB), KUSA
Height 9½–12 in (24–30cm)
Weight 13–16 lb (6–7.5kg)
Coat Profuse, harsh but not coarse, with short, soft, close undercoat; weather-resistant
Color Cream, wheaten, red, gray, or nearly black; brindling acceptable in all these colors; not solid black, solid white, nor black and tan; dark points, such as ears and muzzle, very typical

This popular Scottish terrier, or one very similar, has been known and used for putting down vermin for 150 years or more. It was named after the cairns (a Scottish word that means a heap or pile of stones) that often harbored vermin. The Cairn Terrier originated in the Western Highlands, where the Skye Terrier is well known. There appears to have been some confusion between the breeds at one time, and the Cairn, predominantly a working breed, used to be known as the Short-haired Skye Terrier.

This intelligent, lively little working terrier is still well able to prove its worth as a dispeller of vermin and is also a popular and affectionate pet. It is hardy and enjoys plenty of exercise though it can adapt to most living situations. The Cairn is an easy dog to show, requiring little grooming other than brushing, combing, and removing of excess feathering.

Eyes Set wide apart

Ears Small and pointed

Head Small

Tail Short, balanced, and well-furnished with hair but not feathery

Body Level back

Norfolk Terrier

This breed was once classified with, and known as, the Norwich Terrier. The drop-eared Norfolk Terrier and the prick-eared Norwich Terrier originated in the East Anglian area of England. Both dogs were known as Norwich Terriers from as early as the 1880s. They were probably a mixture of Cairn, Border, and Irish Terriers, and their litters contained both prick-eared and drop-eared varieties. The only difference between the Norfolk and Norwich today is still their ears.

A sociable dog, this hardy, lovable terrier is alert and fearless, but it is good with children, has an equable temperament, and makes a fine pet for those prepared to exercise it. It enjoys a day's rabbiting, and honorable scars are not a drawback in the show ring. It requires daily brushing, and some trimming is all the preparation that is needed for exhibition.

Care requirements

4	3	2	1	🐕
4	3	2	1	🥣
4	3	2	1	🪮
4	3	2	1	🏠

Pedigree points

Recognized AKC, ANKC, CKC, FCI, KC(GB), KUSA
Height 10 in (25.5cm)
Weight 11–12 lb (5–5.5kg)
Coat Hard, wiry, and straight
Color All shades of red, wheaten, black and tan, or grizzle; white marks and patches undesirable but permissible

Eyes Deep-set and oval-shaped

Head Broad skull

Ears Medium-sized, V-shaped, and slightly rounded at tip

Tail Docking optional

Body Compact

Norwich Terrier

From 1964 in Britain, and from 1979 in the United States, the prick-eared Norwich Terrier has been classified separately from the otherwise identical drop-eared Norfolk Terrier. The Norwich Terrier is named after the city of Norwich, which lies in the county of Norfolk in the East Anglian area of eastern England. The Norwich appears to have originated in East Anglia, and probably includes Cairn, Border, and Irish Terrier blood.

This hardy and adaptable terrier is usually good with children. It enjoys regular exercise and needs only a daily brushing for its role as housepet and some trimming in preparation for show.

Care requirements

🐕 1 2 3 4

🥣 1 2 3 4

🖌 1 2 3 4

🏠 1 2 3 4

Pedigree points

Recognized AKC, ANKC, CKC, FCI, KC(GB), KUSA
Height 10 in (25.5cm)
Weight 10–12 lb (4.5–5.5kg)
Coat Hard, wiry, and straight
Color All shades of red, wheaten, black and tan, or grizzle; white marks and patches undesirable

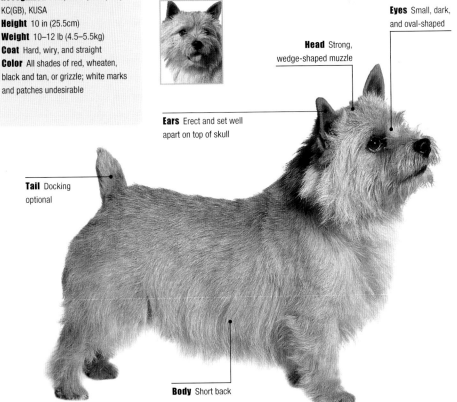

Eyes Small, dark, and oval-shaped

Head Strong, wedge-shaped muzzle

Ears Erect and set well apart on top of skull

Tail Docking optional

Body Short back

Dandie Dinmont Terrier

The Dandie Dinmont Terrier is generally believed to be a relative of the Skye Terrier and was originally bred to hunt badgers and foxes. The novelist Sir Walter Scott included a character called Dandie Dinmont, a farmer with a pack of little terriers, in his novel *Guy Mannering* (1814). Thereafter, the dogs became known as Dandie Dinmont's Terriers, and, in time, as Dandie Dinmonts.

Now kept mainly as a pet, the Dandie Dinmont makes a most affectionate, playful, and intelligent companion, and is in its element as the family's sole pet. It will be happy with as much exercise as its owner is able to provide. This breed is fairly simple to groom, the use of a stiff brush and comb, and the removal of surplus hair, being all that is necessary.

Care requirements

4	3	2	1	🐕
4	3	2	1	🥣
4	3	2	1	🪮
4	3	2	1	🏠

Pedigree points

Recognized AKC, ANKC, CKC, FCI, KC(GB), KUSA
Height 8–11 in (20–27.5cm)
Weight 18–24 lb (8–11kg)
Coat Soft, linty undercoat and harder top coat, not wiry and feeling crisp to the hand
Color Pepper (from bluish black to pale silvery gray) or mustard (from reddish brown to pale fawn)

Eyes Rich, dark hazel

Head Strongly made and large, but in proportion to dog's size

Ears Pendulous

Tail Tapering

Body Long, strong, and flexible

Scottish Terrier

Pedigree points

Recognized AKC, ANKC, CKC, FCI, KC(GB), KUSA
Height 10–11 in (25.5–28cm)
Weight 19–23 lb (8.5–10.5kg)
Coat Sharp, dense, and wiry, with a short, dense, soft undercoat
Color Black, wheaten, or brindle of any shade

The Scottish Terrier or Scottie was once known as the Aberdeen Terrier, after the Scottish city. Like the Cairn, it was bred with the express purpose of dispelling vermin. The Scottie has existed for many centuries and taken many different forms. Indeed, at the end of the 19th century, it was exhibited alongside the Skye, Dandie Dinmont, and West Highland White Terrier under the classification Scotch Terriers.

The Scottie tends to be a one- or two-person dog, perhaps at its best as the pampered pet of a childless couple. It has a reliable temperament but does not welcome interlopers and has no interest in anyone outside its own human family. It enjoys walks, loves to play ball games, and is thoroughly sporty, home-loving, and independent. The Scottie requires daily brushing. Its beard needs gentle brushing and combing, and its coat should be trimmed twice a year.

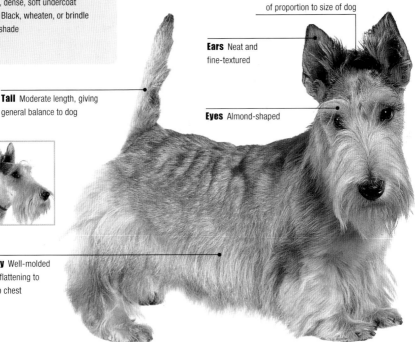

Head Long without being out of proportion to size of dog

Ears Neat and fine-textured

Tail Moderate length, giving general balance to dog

Eyes Almond-shaped

Body Well-molded ribs flattening to deep chest

Sealyham Terrier

Freeman Lloyd, an authority on the Sealyham Terrier, has traced the breed back to the 15th century, when a family called Tucker is reputed to have imported a small, white, long-backed Flemish terrier into Wales. One of the Tuckers' descendants, the sportsman Captain Edwardes, wanted dogs that would hunt with hounds and go to ground in the now illegal sport of badger digging. In the 1880s, he developed the Sealyham from various terrier breeds. The breed took its name from the village of Sealyham near Haverfordwest, Wales, where it was created.

The Sealyham makes a fine show dog and family pet. It is good with children, but not averse to a scrap with its fellows. This breed requires regular brushing and must be hand-stripped for the show ring. If intending to exhibit, advice on grooming should be sought from the breeder or some other expert.

Care requirements

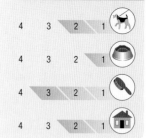

4   3   2   1

4   3   2   1

4   3   2   1

4   3   2   1

Pedigree points

Recognized AKC, ANKC, CKC, FCI, KC(GB), KUSA
Height 12 in (31cm)
Weight Dog: 20 lb (9kg)
Bitch: 18 lb (8kg)
Coat Long, hard, and wiry, with a weather-resistant undercoat
Color All white, or white with lemon, brown, blue, or badger pied markings on head and ears; much black or heavy ticking undesirable

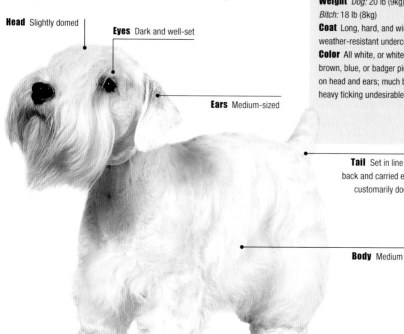

Head Slightly domed

Eyes Dark and well-set

Ears Medium-sized

Tail Set in line with back and carried erect, customarily docked

Body Medium length

Skye Terrier

Care requirements

![dog icon] 1 2 3 4

![bowl icon] 1 2 3 4

![brush icon] 1 2 3 4

![house icon] 1 2 3 4

Pedigree points

Recognized AKC, ANKC, CKC, FCI, KC(GB), KUSA
Height *Dog:* 10 in (25cm)
Bitch: 9½ in (24cm)
Weight 25 lb (11.3kg)
Coat Long, hard, straight, flat, and free from curl, with a short, close, soft, woolly undercoat
Color Black, dark or light gray, fawn or cream, all with black points

The Skye developed from small dogs kept in the Highlands of Scotland to go to ground after badger, fox, otter, and rabbit. The best of these "earth" terriers were said to originate in the Isle of Skye. For a considerable time, the Skye and Cairn Terriers were thought to be one breed, the Cairn being described as a Short-haired Skye. There were also Skyes with drop and pricked ears. Probably the most famous Skye Terrier is Greyfriars Bobby, the subject of a romantic tale. In the 1850s, Bobby's master died and was buried in the graveyard of Greyfriars' Church in Edinburgh. Bobby lay on his master's grave for 14 years until his own death. A statue to commemorate Bobby's faithfullness stands near Greyfriars' Church.

The Skye Terrier tends to be suspicious of or uninterested in anyone other than its owner. Its magnificent long coat requires a considerable amount of grooming, particularly as this little dog enjoys country walks.

Eyes Brown and preferably dark

Head Long and powerful

Ears Pricked or drop

Tail Upper part pendulous, lower part thrown back in a curve when hanging, and looks like extension of the back line when raised

Body Long and low with level back

West Highland White Terrier

Like other small Scottish terriers, the West Highland White Terrier or Westie was bred to hunt vermin. At one time it was classed along with the Cairn and Skye Terriers as a Small Highland Working Terrier. The Westie has also gone under a number of other names. In the late 1800s, there was a strain of white Scottish Terriers owned by Colonel Malcolm of Poltalloch and known as Poltalloch Terriers. A picture of Colonel Malcolm with his dogs reveals that they were not all that different from the Westie we know today. Dogs of this type were also known as Roseneath Terriers or White Roseneath Terriers, and in a breed supplement published in 1899, they were classified as a subvariety of the Scottish Terrier. Today, the Westie is among the most popular of purebred dogs.

The Westie is described in its standard as being "possessed of no small amount of self-esteem with a varminty appearance." This game and hardy little terrier is easy to train, gets on well with children, and is a suitable housepet for people in town as well as in the country. Regular brushing keeps the white coat clean, but stripping and trimming are required for show, and if it is the intention to exhibit, advice on preparation should be sought from the breeder.

Undeniably cute with its pricked ears and black button nose, the Westie is nonetheless a game little terrier well able to perform in the field, where its white coat makes it more easily distinguished from game than other terriers.

Head Slightly domed

Eyes Set wide apart

Tail 5–6 in
(12.5–15cm) long

Ears Small, erect,
and carried firmly

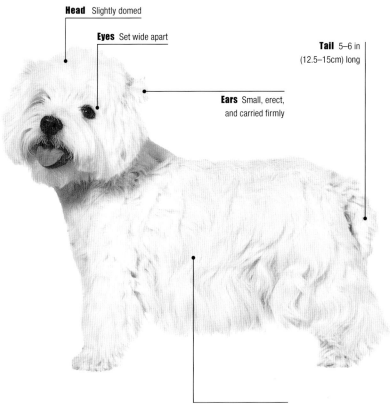

Body Compact with level
back and broad, strong loins

Pedigree points

Recognized AKC, ANKC, CKC, FCI,
KC(GB), KUSA
Height *Dog:* 11 in (27.5cm)
Bitch: 10 in (25cm)
Weight 15–22 lb (7–10kg)
Coat Harsh and free from curl, with
a short, soft, close furry undercoat
Color White

Care requirements

	1	2	3	4
	1	2	3	4
	1	2	3	4
	1	2	3	4

Czesky Terrier

The Czesky or Bohemian Terrier is a short-legged terrier, little known outside its native home of the Czech Republic. It was developed in the middle of this century by crossing the Scottish, Sealyham, and possibly other terriers. The result is a tough, sturdy dog that will go to ground after quarry, and is an excellent ratter and guard.

As well as being a fine working terrier, the Czesky's equable temperament also makes it a good children's companion. It requires plenty of exercise and expert clipping for the show ring, although pet owners could probably get away with the occasional visit to the grooming parlor and a good daily brushing.

Care requirements

4	3	2	1
4	3	2	1
4	3	2	1
4	3	2	1

Pedigree points

Recognized FCI, KC(GB)
Height 11–14 in (28–35.5cm)
Weight 13–20 lb (6–9kg)
Coat Fine and silky, with tendency to curl
Color Blue-gray or brown with light markings

Eyes Deep-set

Head Long

Ears Pendant

Tail 7–8 in (17.5–20cm) long, carried horizontally when excited

Body Sturdy

Australian Terrier

Pedigree points

Recognized AKC, ANKC, CKC, FCI, KC(GB), KUSA

Height 10–11 in (25–27.5cm)

Weight 14 lb (6.5kg)

Coat Harsh, straight, dense, and long, with short, soft undercoat

Color *A:* blue, steel blue, or dark gray-blue with rich tan (not sandy) on face, ears, under body, lower legs, and around the vent (puppies excepted); topknot blue or silver, of a lighter shade than leg color *B:* clear sandy or red; smuttiness or dark shadings undesirable; topknot a lighter shade

The Australian Terrier is often mistaken for a large Yorkshire Terrier. This is not surprising since it is considered to result from the mating of a Yorkshire Terrier bitch and a dog that resembled a Cairn Terrier. By the time the breed was first exhibited in 1899, it had been in existence for about 20 years and was reputed to be an unsurpassed vermin killer that could also dispose of a snake.

After a slow start, this breed is now proving a popular dog outside its native Australia, both in the international show ring and as an alert, hardy, and devoted family pet. The Australian needs only a good daily grooming with a bristle brush. Since it has a weather-resistant coat, it may be kenneled outdoors, though most owners do keep them indoors.

Eyes Small

Ears Small, erect, and pointed

Head Long with flat skull and powerful jaw

Tail Set high and customarily docked

Body Long in proportion to height

Toy Breeds

Affenpinscher

The Affenpinscher is the smallest of the pinschers and schnauzers. Its name comes from its monkey-like face (the German *affen* means "monkeys"). It is also known in its native country as the Dwarf Pinscher, and in France as the Diabletin Moustache ("the moustached little devil"). It greatly resembles the Brussels Griffon, but whether it was the Griffon that contributed to the Affenpinscher or vice versa is debatable.

This appealing, naturally scruffy-looking toy dog has a keen intelligence and is exceedingly affectionate. It makes a good watchdog and, terrier-like, is not averse to rabbiting. Its thick coat benefits from being brushed daily.

Care requirements

Pedigree points

Recognized AKC, ANKC, CKC, FCI, KC (GB), KUSA
Height 9½–11 in (24–28cm)
Weight 6½–9 lb (3–4kg)
Coat Rough and thick
Color Preferably black, but gray shading permissible

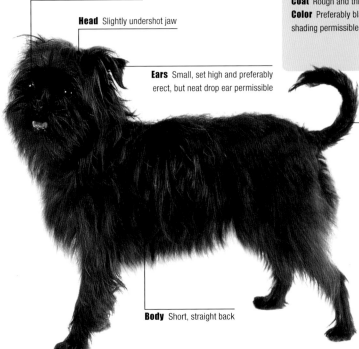

Eyes Round, dark, and sparkling

Head Slightly undershot jaw

Ears Small, set high and preferably erect, but neat drop ear permissible

Tail Set high and docked in some countries

Body Short, straight back

Care requirements

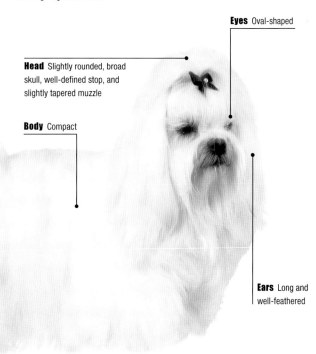

1 2 3 4

1 2 3 4

1 2 3 4

1 2 3 4

Pedigree points

Recognized AKC, ANKC, CKC, FCI, KC(GB), KUSA
Height 10 in (25.5cm) maximum
Weight 7 lb (3kg) maximum
Coat Long, straight, and silky
Color White; slight lemon markings on ears permissible

Maltese

A member of the bichon family, this small, white dog is one of the oldest European breeds. It has existed on the island of Malta for centuries, and also found its way to China and the Philippines via Maltese traders. However, in about AD 25, the Greek historian Strabo reported: "There is a town in Sicily called Melita whence are exported many beautiful dogs called Canis Melitei," raising the possibility of Italian origin for the breed.

The long-established Maltese seems to have been overtaken in popularity by other toys, and is now seldom seen outside the show ring. This is unfortunate because it is a happy, healthy, long-lived little dog that is good with children and makes a lovable pet. It is fairly adaptable as far as exercise is concerned, but requires grooming every day with a bristle brush. Owners are advised to check with the breeder about show preparation.

Eyes Oval-shaped

Head Slightly rounded, broad skull, well-defined stop, and slightly tapered muzzle

Body Compact

Tail Long, plumed, and carried arched over back

Ears Long and well-feathered

Löwchen

The Löwchen is also known as the Little Lion Dog because it was traditionally given a lion clip, similar to that sported by the exhibition poodle. Complete with mane and tufted tail, the Löwchen does look like a lion in miniature. This breed is a member of the bichon family, and is thought to have originated in the Mediterranean area. It is recognized as a French breed, but has been known in both France and Spain since the late 1500s. The Löwchen is widely believed to be the dog included by the Spanish artist, Francisco de Goya, in a painting of his friend, the Duchess of Alba.

The Löwchen is an affectionate, intelligent dog that is popular in the show ring but rarely seen walking in the park. It enjoys life as a pet given the chance, and is a lively animal, requiring daily brushing. If it is your intention to exhibit your Löwchen, expert advice on clipping should be sought.

Care requirements

4	3	2	1
4	3	2	1
4	3	2	1
4	3	2	1

Pedigree points

Recognized ANKC, FCI, KC(GB), KUSA
Height 10–13 in (25–33cm)
Weight 8–18 lb (3.5–8kg)
Coat Moderately long and wavy
Color Any color or combination of colors permissible

Eyes Round and dark with intelligent expression

Head Wide, short skull

Ears Long, pendant, and well-fringed

Tail Medium length and clipped to resemble a plume

Body Strong and short

Brussels Griffon

Pedigree points

Recognized AKC, ANKC, CKC, FCI, KC(GB), KUSA
Height 7–8 in (18–20.5cm)
Weight 5–11 lb (2.2–5kg), but 6–10 lb (2.7–4.5kg) most desirable
Coat *Rough:* harsh and wiry
Smooth: soft and smooth
Color Red, black, or black and rich tan with white markings; FCI classifies the black, black/tan, or red/black as Belgian Griffon

An early example of the Brussels Griffon is depicted in a painting of 1434 by the Flemish painter, Jan Van Eyck. Once kept by hansom cab drivers of 17th-century Brussels to rid their stables of vermin, the Brussels Griffon became a companion breed by virtue of its appealing character. When Pug blood was added to the rough-coated Brussels Griffon, the infusion resulted in a smooth-haired variety, which is recognized as a distinct breed in Europe known as the Petit Brabançon. Other breeds, including Yorkshire and Irish Terriers, have undoubtedly contributed to the modern griffons.

This intelligent, cheerful little dog, with its terrier-like disposition, makes a fine companion. The Griffon has never suffered from the overpopularity of some breeds and is a good family choice. The coat of the rough requires a lot of attention, but the coats of pet dogs may be clipped.

Ears Large, prominent, and set well apart

Head Large in comparison to body, rounded but in no way domed, and wide between the ears

Eyes Black rimmed and very dark

Tail Carried high and customarily docked

Body Short back, level from withers to tail root, neither roaching nor dipping

English Toy Terrier

The English Toy Terrier was bred from the Manchester Terrier. This larger but otherwise similar breed was developed from the now extinct rough-haired Black and Tan Terrier and other breeds. The Italian Greyhound and, possibly, the Whippet may also have contributed to the English Toy Terrier. The Manchester Terrier was bred to kill rats in a pit for public entertainment, and its smaller relative is an excellent ratter.

Surprisingly rare outside the show ring today, the English Toy Terrier still retains the ability to hunt vermin and makes an affectionate and intelligent companion. It is good with children but tends to be a one-person dog. The English Toy is easy to care for, requiring little more than a daily brushing and a rub-down to give its coat a sheen. It is a reasonably tough little dog and does not have quite the same aversion to rain as its more fastidious Italian Greyhound relatives.

Care requirements

4	3	2	1
4	3	2	1
4	3	2	1
4	3	2	1

Pedigree points

Recognized AKC, ANKC, CKC, FCI, KC(GB), KUSA
Height 10–12 in (25–30cm)
Weight 6–9 lb (2.5–3.5kg)
Coat Thick, close, and glossy
Color Black and tan

Head Long and narrow

Ears Candle flame-shaped and slightly pointed at tips

Eyes Dark to black

Tail Thick at root and tapering to a point

Body Compact

Yorkshire Terrier

Care requirements

1 2 3 4

1 2 3 4

1 2 3 4

1 2 3 4

Pedigree points

Recognized AKC, ANKC, CKC, FCI, KC(GB), KUSA
Height 9 in (22cm)
Weight 7 lb (3kg) maximum
Coat Glossy, fine, and silky
Color Dark steel blue (not silver blue) extending from back of head to root of tail, never mingled with fawn, bronze, or dark hairs; face, chest, and feet rich, bright tan

The Yorkshire Terrier or Yorkie is a comparatively recent breed, having been developed in Yorkshire, England, within the last hundred years through the crossing of a Skye Terrier and the extinct Black and Tan Terrier, a forerunner of the Manchester Terrier. The Maltese and Dandie Dinmont may also have contributed to its make-up. The Yorkie is seen in many different sizes and people often think there are two varieties, miniature and standard. In fact, the Yorkie should not exceed 7 lb (3kg), making it one of the world's smallest dogs. There are, however, many larger specimens that are ideal as pets.

The Yorkie is suited to town or country living, and like most small terriers, is utterly fearless. This bossy, inordinately affectionate and lively little dog makes a fine pet. It is also a first-class show dog for those with the time to spare for intricate grooming.

Head Small and flat on top

Ears Small, V-shaped, and carried erect

Eyes Medium-sized, dark, and sparkling

Tail Medium length and usually docked

Body Compact

Australian Silky Terrier

The Australian Silky Terrier, or Silky Terrier, was originally known as the Sydney Silky, and the progeny were registered under that name as recently as 1945. It owes its existence to the cross-breeding of Skye and Yorkshire Terriers, and also of the Yorkshire and Australian Terriers (the Australian having not only Yorkie but Dandie Dinmont, Cairn, and Norwich terrier blood in its veins). The first breed standard was not published until 1962, although the breed was accepted in the United States three years earlier.

The Australian Silky is a typical terrier in temperament. It is not averse to a spot of vermin hunting but offers its owners much affection. It needs good daily walks to work off its energy and regular brushing and combing—lots of attention to its coat is essential if it is to compete in the show ring.

The Australian Silky Terrier probably traces its sheen back to the Dandie Dinmont, an early 19th-century ancestor that contributed to the line. Unlike that of the Yorkie (another ancestor), the Silky's coat stops short of the ground, leaving the paws visible.

Head Medium length

Ears Small and V-shaped

Tail Customarily docked

Eyes Small, dark, and round

Body Small, compactly built, with body slightly longer than height

Pedigree points

Recognized AKC, ANKC, CKC, FCI, KC(GB), KUSA
Height 9 in (22.5cm)
Weight 8–10 lb (3.5–4.5kg)
Coat Straight, fine, and glossy
Color Blue and tan, gray, or blue and tan with silver-blue topknot; tips of hairs should be darker at roots

Care requirements

	1	2	3	4
	1	2	3	4
	1	2	3	4
	1	2	3	4

Pug

It is likely that the Pug originated in China, and it may be a greatly scaled-down relative of the Tibetan Mastiff. By the 1500s, it had been taken on trading ships to Holland, where it became popular with the royal family of the time, the House of Orange, and is often referred to as the Dutch Pug. The breed is generally believed to have been introduced into Britain in 1688 by William, Prince of Orange, who became William III of Britain. During William's reign, the Pug is said to have enjoyed unrivaled status. By 1790, it reached France, where a favorite Pug of Empress Josephine is alleged to have bitten Napoleon on their wedding night.

This happy, intelligent little dog is good with children, and requires only modest exercise, but the Pug should not be exercised in very hot weather. Daily grooming with a brush and a rub-down with a silk handkerchief will make its coat shine.

Care requirements

4	3	2	1
4	3	2	1
4	3	2	1
4	3	2	1

Pedigree points

Recognized AKC, ANKC, CKC, FCI, KC(GB), KUSA
Height 10–12 in (25–27.5cm)
Weight 14–18 lb (6.5–8kg)
Coat Fine, smooth, short, and glossy
Color Silver, apricot, fawn, or black; black mask and ears and black trace along back

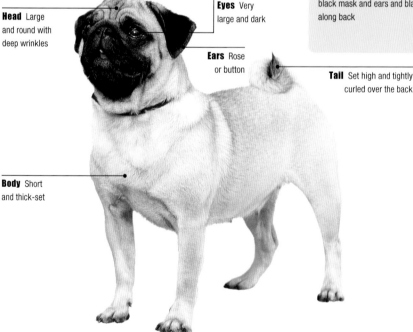

Head Large and round with deep wrinkles

Eyes Very large and dark

Ears Rose or button

Tail Set high and tightly curled over the back

Body Short and thick-set

Pomeranian

Care requirements

1	2	3	4
1	2	3	4
1	2	3	4
1	2	3	4

Pedigree points

Recognized AKC, ANKC, CKC, KC(GB), KUSA
Height 11 in (27.5cm) maximum
Weight 3–7 lb (1.5–3kg)
Coat Long, straight, and harsh, with a soft, fluffy undercoat
Color All colors permissible, but free from black or white shadings; whole colors are white, black, brown, or light or dark blue

This small dog is a member of the spitz family, and like other spitz, originated in the Arctic Circle. The Pomeranian derives from white spitz that existed in Pomerania, northern Germany, from about 1700. They were much larger dogs and were bred down after being imported into Britain about a hundred years ago. Queen Victoria was much taken with the breed, which helped to make it very popular.

The Pomeranian seems to have gained the reputation of being an old lady's lapdog. While it is certainly ideal for that role, adoring lots of attention, it is also a lively, robust little dog that would walk its owners off their feet if given the chance. This affectionate and faithful dog is good with children and makes a delightful pet. It is also a fine show dog for those with plenty of time on their hands to care for its double coat, which must be groomed with a stiff brush every day and regularly trimmed.

Ears Small, erect, and set not too low down or too wide apart

Head Soft in outline

Tail Set high, turning over back, and carried flat and straight

Body Short back and compact body

Eyes Medium-sized

Papillon

The Papillon is also known as the Continental Toy Spaniel. The name Papillon, which is French for "butterfly," comes from the breed's erect ears. An identical drop-eared variety is known as the Phalène or "moth." The Papillon has often been mistaken for the Long-coated Chihuahua, a variety it helped to produce. In fact, the Papillon originated in Spain and is said to be a descendant of the 16th-century Dwarf Spaniel. It has been included in paintings by Rubens and Van Dyke. Like the toy spaniels and the Maltese, the Papillon became a favorite of the aristocracy wherever it went.

The Papillon is intelligent, usually healthy, and has proved an able contender in obedience competitions. It is fairly easy to look after, needing only a daily brushing to keep the coat shining.

Care requirements

4	3	2	1
4	3	2	1
4	3	2	1
4	3	2	1

Pedigree points

Recognized AKC, ANKC, CKC, FCI, KC(GB), KUSA
Height 8–11 in (20–28cm)
Coat Long, abundant, flowing, and silky
Color White with patches of any color except liver; tricolor: black and white with tan in spots over eyes and inside ears, on cheeks, and under root of tail

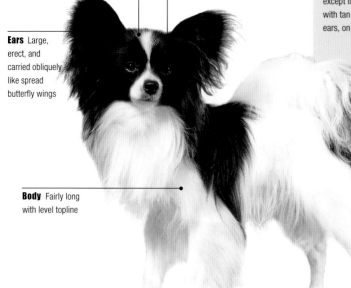

Head Slightly rounded

Eyes Dark and medium-sized

Ears Large, erect, and carried obliquely like spread butterfly wings

Tail Long and well-fringed

Body Fairly long with level topline

Pekingese

Pedigree points

Recognized AKC, ANKC, CKC, FCI, KC(GB), KUSA

Weight *Dog:* 11 lb (5kg) maximum
Bitch: 12 lb (5.5kg) maximum

Coat Long, straight double coat with coarse top coat and thick undercoat; profuse mane and feathered tail

Color All colors and marking are permissible and of equal merit, except albino or liver; particolors should be evenly broken

The origins of the Pekingese may trace back some 1,500 years. Believed to be a close relative of the Lhasa Apso and Shih Tzu, the Pekingese was said to combine the nobility of the lion with the grace and sweetness of the marmoset. Favored by the 19th-century Chinese imperial court, they were kept in their thousands in extraordinarily privileged circumstances. The Pekingese first arrived in Europe and the US when some Western countries, including the UK and the US, raided the Summer Palace in Peking following the Boxer Rebellion of 1860. The soldiers found five imperial Pekingese and these were taken to England.

The Pekingese is a thick-set, dignified little dog with a mind of its own and is good with adults and children. Intelligent and fearless, it does not mind walking across a muddy field but its ideal role is that of a pampered, sole companion. It requires considerable brushing and combing.

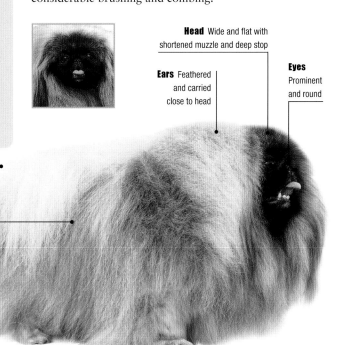

Head Wide and flat with shortened muzzle and deep stop

Ears Feathered and carried close to head

Eyes Prominent and round

Tail Set high and curving over back

Body Pear-shaped and compact

Japanese Chin

There are two theories on the origin of the Japanese Chin or Japanese Spaniel. One is that it derives from Pekingese-like dogs brought to Japan by Zen Buddhist monks in the AD 500s, and the other that it descends from a lapdog sent as a present in AD 732 to the Emperor of Japan from Korea. It is not dissimilar to the Pekingese, but is longer in the leg and lighter. Whatever its ancestry, for more than 1,000 years this little dog was a favorite of Japanese emperors who decreed that it should be worshiped. It is said that smaller Chins were sometimes kept in hanging cages like pet birds. Two Japanese Chins were presented to Queen Victoria by Commodore Perry, an American naval commander, on his return from the Far East in 1853.

Bearing some resemblance to the King Charles Spaniel, the Chin is a popular show dog but less often kept as a pet. This attractive and hardy little dog is good with children. It requires an average amount of exercise and little grooming, except for a daily going over with a pure-bristle brush. Like other flat-nosed breeds, it must not be over-exerted in hot weather lest it should suffer breathing difficulties.

The Japanese Chin probably shares a common ancestor with the Pekingese and the Pug. The Chin is longer in the leg than the Pekingese and lighter in color, and both dogs were once revered by the nobility.

Head Large, round, in proportion to size of dog, and with short muzzle

Eyes Large and dark

Ears Small and set wide apart

Body Square and compact

Tail Well-feathered, set high, and curling over back

Pedigree points

Recognized AKC, ANKC, CKC, FCI, KC(GB), KUSA
Weight 4–7 lb (2–3kg)
Coat Profuse, long, soft, and straight
Color White and black or white and red (all shades, including sable, lemon, and orange); never tricolor

Care requirements

	1	2	3	4
🐕	1	2	3	4
🥣	1	2	3	4
🪮	1	2	3	4
🏠	1	2	3	4

King Charles Spaniel

In North America, this breed is known as the English Toy Spaniel and the name "King Charles" is given to the Black and Tan variety only. Although the King Charles Spaniel is generally thought of as a British breed, its history traces back to Japan in 2000 BC. It is said that King Charles II was so devoted to these little spaniels that he would frequently interrupt affairs of state in order to fondle and play with them, and there is a law in England, yet to be rescinded, that enables a King Charles Spaniel "to go anywhere."

This little spaniel makes a delightful pet, being good with children, full of fun, and able to adapt its exercise requirements to its owner's capabilities. The King Charles should be brushed every day with a bristle brush, and it is advisable to keep the area around its eyes clean with eye wipes.

Care requirements

4	3	2	1
4	3	2	1
4	3	2	1
4	3	2	1

Pedigree points

Recognized AKC, ANKC, CKC, FCI, KC(GB), KUSA

Height 10 in (25cm)

Weight 8–14 lb (3.5–6.5kg)

Coat Long, silky, and straight; slight waviness permissible

Color *Black and Tan:* black with tan marks above eyes, on cheeks, inside ears, on chest and legs, and underside of tail; white marks undesirable *Ruby:* solid rich red; white marks undesirable *Blenheim:* chestnut markings, well broken up, on pearly white ground; markings evenly divided on head, lozenge spot between ears *Tricolor:* black and white, well-spaced and broken up, with tan marks over eyes, cheeks, inside ears, inside legs, and underside of tail

Head Large, domed skull, full over eyes, and a deep, well-defined stop

Tail Well-feathered, docked in the US

Eyes Large and dark

Ears Long, well-feathered, and set low

Body Wide, deep chest

Care requirements

1 2 3 4

1 2 3 4

1 2 3 4

1 2 3 4

Pedigree points

Recognized ANKC, CKC, FCI, KC(GB), KUSA.

Weight 12–18 lb (5.5–8kg)

Coat Long, silky, and free from curl

Color *Black and Tan:* black with bright tan marks above eyes, head, chest, legs, underside of tail; white marks undesirable *Ruby:* rich red; white markings undesirable *Blenheim:* chestnut markings, well broken up, on white ground; markings evenly divided on head, lozenge between ears *Tricolor:* black and white, well-spaced and broken up, with tan markings over head, inside legs, and underside of tail

Cavalier King Charles Spaniel

The Cavalier King Charles Spaniel originated in Japan, and there is a resemblance between it and the Japanese Chin. The Cavalier is very similar to the King Charles Spaniel, but while the King Charles has an apple-domed head, the slightly larger Cavalier is almost flat between the ears and its stop is shallower. Both breeds were named after Charles II and the Cavalier was the original favorite. Today, the Cavalier is one of the most popular pet dogs, although it is not recognized as a separate breed in the US.

This breed is an admirable choice of family pet, being good natured and fond of children. While it is allocated to the toy group, it is among the largest of the toys and enjoys a fair amount of exercise. It should be groomed every day with a bristle brush.

Eyes Large and dark

Head Flattish skull

Ears Long and set high

Tail Long and well-feathered

Body Short-coupled

Chihuahua

The Chihuahua, the smallest dog in the world, is named after the state of Chihuahua in Mexico and is believed by some to have been a sacred dog of the Aztecs. However, a dog not unlike the Chihuahua may well have existed in Egypt some 3,000 years ago. In 1910, a zoologist found the mummified remains of a little dog in an Egyptian tomb that had the soft spot in the skull that is common in the breed. Chihuahuas have been known in Malta for many centuries, having arrived there from North Africa around 600 BC, and a Botticelli fresco (c.1482) in the Sistine Chapel in Rome includes the likeness of a Chihuahua. There are two varieties of Chihuahua: the Smooth-coated and Long-coated, the latter having long hair of soft texture that is either flat or slightly wavy.

The Chihuahua is an exceedingly intelligent dog that is affectionate, possessive, and makes a good watchdog in miniature. Despite being generally thought of as a lapdog, it can walk as far as most owners would wish. Care must be taken on outings that it does not start a fight because it seems to imagine that it is enormous when confronted with other canines. The breed is expensive to keep, and both Long-haireds and Smooth-haireds are fairly easy to groom, requiring only daily combing and brushing with a soft brush.

Smooth-coated Chihuahua

At one time the two varieties of Chihuahua—Long-coated and Smooth-coated—were allowed to interbreed, but this is no longer acceptable.

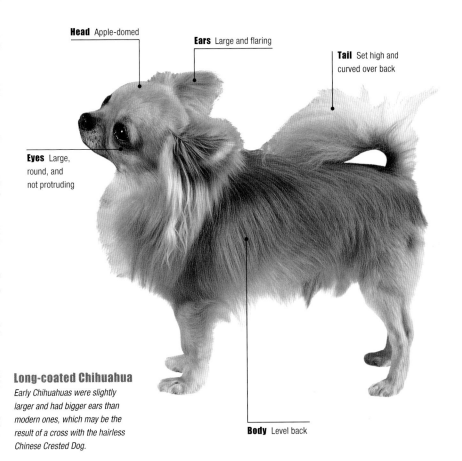

Head Apple-domed

Ears Large and flaring

Tail Set high and curved over back

Eyes Large, round, and not protruding

Body Level back

Long-coated Chihuahua

Early Chihuahuas were slightly larger and had bigger ears than modern ones, which may be the result of a cross with the hairless Chinese Crested Dog.

Pedigree points

Recognized AKC, ANKC, CKC, FCI, KC(GB), KUSA
Height 6.5–8 in (16–20cm)
Weight 6 lb (2.7kg) maximum
Coat *Long-coated:* long and soft to touch, slight waviness permissible
Smooth-coated: short and dense, soft to touch
Color Any color or mixture

Care requirements

	1	2	3	4
	1	2	3	4
	1	2	3	4
	1	2	3	4

Italian Greyhound

There is little doubt that the Italian Greyhound is a descendant of the Greyhound, but there appears to be no record of how and when it was reduced in size. The Greyhound is one of the most ancient breeds in the world, depicted in the tombs of the Egyptian pharaohs; drawings of smaller Greyhounds also date back to Egyptian and Roman times.

The Italian Greyhound is a delightful, affectionate housepet that is easy to train, rarely molts, and is odorless. However, this dainty little dog is very sensitive. It feels the cold, can be wounded by harsh words, and its legs are easily broken. The breed enjoys a fair amount of exercise, but must have a warm coat in wintry conditions. It is easy to groom, a rub-down with a silk handkerchief making its coat shine.

Care requirements

4	3	2	1
4	3	2	1
4	3	2	1
4	3	2	1

Pedigree points

Recognized AKC, ANKC, CKC, FCI, KC (GB), KUSA
Height 12½–15 in (32–38cm)
Weight 5½–10 lb (2.5–4.5kg)
Coat Short, fine, and glossy
Color Solid black, blue, cream, fawn, red, or white, or any of these colors broken with white; white broken with one of the above colors; black or blue with tan markings, or brindle, not acceptable

Head Long, flat, and narrow with a slight stop

Ears Rose-shaped and set well back

Eyes Large and expressive

Tail Long, set low, and carried low

Body Deep, narrow chest

Miniature Pinscher

Pedigree points

Recognized AKC, ANKC, CKC, FCI, KC(GB), KUSA

Height 10–12 in (25.5–30cm)

Weight 10 lb (4.5kg)

Coat Hard, smooth, and short

Color Black, blue, or chocolate, with sharply defined tan markings on cheeks, lips, lower jaw, throat, twin spots above eyes and cheeks, lower half of forelegs, inside of hind legs and vent region, lower portion of nodes, and feet

The Miniature Pinscher, or Min Pin as it is commonly called, is not, as many believe, a small Doberman. Its ancestor is the German Pinscher to which Italian Greyhound and, it is thought, Dachshund blood were added. A painting, *The Peasant Family*, dated 1640 and currently in the Louvre, Paris, includes the likeness of a dog similar to the Miniature Pinscher.

The Min Pin has an attractive hackney (high-stepping) gait. It makes an ideal pet for town or country, being affectionate and intelligent, and rarely molting. The breed enjoys obedience work and exercise, often following a scent. It is easy to groom, requiring little more than a daily brush and a rub-down with a silk handkerchief or piece of chamois leather to make its coat shine.

Head Tapering, narrow skull

Ears Small, set high, and erect or dropped

Tail Set high, level with topline, and often docked

Eyes Bright and dark

Body Compact and square

Chinese Crested Dog

The almost hairless Chinese Crested is said to have originated in China and been taken to South America in Chinese sailing ships many centuries ago. However, there have been hairless dogs in many countries of the world, including Africa and Turkey, and some think the Chinese Crested may be the result of the mating of a Mexican Hairless Dog with the Chihuahua. Certainly the mating of a Chinese Crested with a Chihuahua can produce a completely hairless dog.

The Chinese Crested has no coat except for a flowing crest or mane, hair on its feet, and a gaily carried, plumed tail. However, in almost every litter, there are some haired pups that grow into luxuriantly coated adults that resemble little sheepdogs. These are known as Powder Puffs.

This affectionate little dog makes an excellent pet for those who appreciate its loving nature and are not put off by its exuberance. It is frequently hyperactive, playing tirelessly and leaping about in circles in anticipation of the tiniest crumb of food. The Chinese Crested adores food, its body feeling hotter to the touch after it has eaten, and rations should be increased in the winter months. Its paws will grip in an endearing, almost human fashion. Ideally, it should be bathed about every three weeks and have its skin massaged with cream. Whiskers, and any straggly odd hairs, should be removed for the show ring. This breed can adjust to warm or cold climates but should never be kenneled outdoors and must be protected against sunburn.

Powder Puff Chinese Crested Dog

The Powder Puff Chinese Crested Dog takes its name from the silky double coat, which makes its ears drop forward.

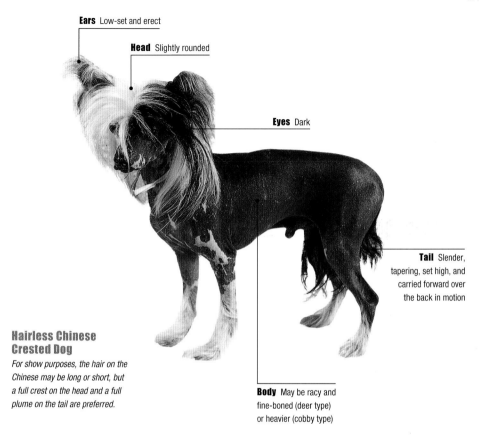

Ears Low-set and erect

Head Slightly rounded

Eyes Dark

Tail Slender, tapering, set high, and carried forward over the back in motion

Body May be racy and fine-boned (deer type) or heavier (cobby type)

Hairless Chinese Crested Dog

For show purposes, the hair on the Chinese may be long or short, but a full crest on the head and a full plume on the tail are preferred.

Pedigree points

Recognized AKC, ANKC, CKC, FCI, KC(GB), KUSA
Height *Dog:* 11–13 in (28–33cm)
Bitch: 9–12 in (23–30.5cm)
Weight 12 lb (5.5kg) maximum
Coat *Hairless:* Tuft of long, soft hair only on head, feet and tail
Powder Puff: Double, long, straight outer coat, soft silky undercoat
Color Any color or combination

Care requirements

	1	2	3	4
	1	2	3	4
	1	2	3	4
	1	2	3	4

Index

Credits

Quarto would like to thank all the owners who kindly allowed us to photograph their dogs for inclusion in this book. All photographs are the copyright of Quarto.